THE
BLACK DEATH

GREAT HISTORIC DISASTERS

THE
BLACK DEATH

LOUISE CHIPLEY SLAVICEK

CHELSEA HOUSE
PUBLISHERS
An imprint of Infobase Publishing

THE BLACK DEATH

Chelsea House
An imprint of Infobase Publishing
132 West 31st Street
New York NY 10001

Library of Congress Cataloging-in-Publication Data
Slavicek, Louise Chipley.
The black death/Louise Chipley Slavicek.
   p.   cm.—(Great historic disasters)
Includes bibliographical references and index.
ISBN: 978-0-7910-9649-9 (hardcover)
1. Black Death. I. Title. II. Series.
RC171.S633 2008
616.9'232—dc22   2008004887

Chelsea House books are available at special discounts when purchased in bulk quantities for businesses, associations, institutions, or sales promotions. Please call our Special Sales Department in New York at (212) 967-8800 or (800) 322-8755.

You can find Chelsea House on the World Wide Web
at http://www.chelseahouse.com

Text design by Annie O'Donnell
Cover design by Ben Peterson

Printed in the United States of America

Bang KT 10 9 8 7 6 5 4 3 2 1

This book is printed on acid-free paper.

All links and Web addresses were checked and verified to be correct at the time of publication. Because of the dynamic nature of the Web, some addresses and links may have changed since publication and may no longer be valid.

Contents

Introduction:
"Life Is But One
Long Agony"

In 1346, Europe was hit by the worst natural disaster in its recorded history: the Black Death. Generally believed to be a combination of bubonic plague and two other plague strains, the Black Death ravaged the length and breadth of Europe from Sicily to Norway, from Ireland to Russia, for five terrible years. Scholars can only speculate regarding how many people perished in the lethal pandemic, which also swept across parts of western Asia and North Africa during the late 1340s and early 1350s. Most historians, however, agree that the Black Death killed anywhere from 33 to 60 percent of Europe's total population—roughly 25 million to 45 million men, women, and children. (A pandemic is a disease outbreak that affects a large geographical area and a high percentage of the population.)

THE GREAT MORTALITY
AND THE BLACK DEATH

During the Middle Ages (about 400 to 1400), the notorious pandemic of the mid-1300s was usually referred to as the Great Mortality or, simply, the pestilence (meaning a deadly contagious disease). The term *Black Death* did not come into

7

The Black Death in Europe, 1347–1352

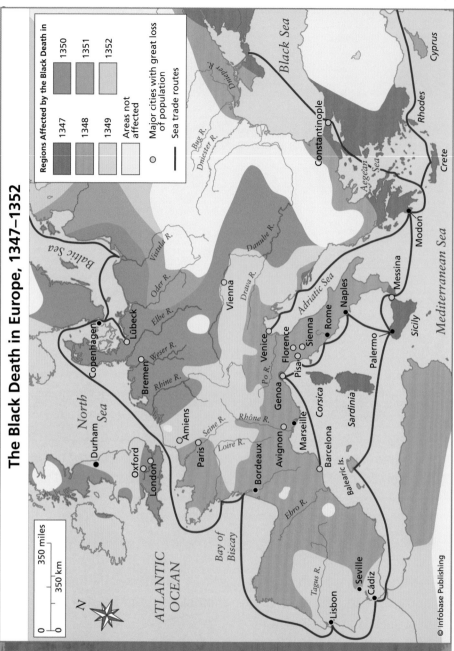

Regions Affected by the Black Death in

- 1347
- 1348
- 1349
- 1350
- 1351
- 1352
- Areas not affected
- ○ Major cities with great loss of population
- — Sea trade routes

© Infobase Publishing

The Black Death is one of history's most devastating plagues. It destroyed between 33 and 60 percent of medieval Europe's population. The spread of the plague has been linked to the growth of international trade between Asia, where the Black Death is believed to have originated.

general use until centuries after the outbreak. To date, just one writing from the medieval era has been found that mentions the phrase—a Latin poem about the pandemic that scholars now believe may have been mistranslated.

In the poem, author Simon de Covinus, a Flemish (Belgian) astronomer, labels the pandemic as the "mors atra." Later European translators of de Covinus's poem, and of several sixteenth-century Swedish and Danish chronicles that use the same term, took the phrase to mean "the black death," even though the word *atra* signifies both "terrible" and "black" in Latin. The translators may have chosen "black" rather than "terrible" as the more likely of the two meanings because they were under the common misconception that the fingers and other extremities of plague victims usually blacken as the disease progresses. In fact, blackening of the extremities from hemorrhaging beneath the skin (heavy bleeding from ruptured blood vessels) only occurs in an extremely rare plague strain known as septicemic plague. Accurate or not, by the early twentieth century the term *Black Death* had become the standard name throughout much of the Western world for what may very well be the greatest medical catastrophe of all time.

A TRAGEDY OF EXTRAORDINARY PROPORTIONS

Today, most scholars concur that the huge population loss caused by the Black Death deeply impacted the course of European history, accelerating and in some instances—initiating—major social, economic, and cultural changes. The psychological toll that the pandemic exacted from those who lived through it was also profound. People were shocked and terrified by the unprecedented scale of the tragedy, which struck young and old, rich and poor, city dwellers and rural folk, with equal ferocity. Seemingly, there was no way to stop the deadly scourge. Nor did anyone have the slightest idea of what lay behind it. Many people concluded that the mysterious illness must have come from God himself—a horrific punishment for humankind's sins.

"Life is but one long agony," the great medieval poet Petrarch (Francesco Petrarca) observed mournfully in 1348 as the Black Death raged through his Italian homeland. In his short Latin poem *Ad Se Ipsum* ("To Himself"), composed that same year, Petrarch (who lost many close friends as well as the woman he loved to the plague) wrote poignantly of the grief and dread that seemed to press in on him from every side:

> *Time rushes onward for the perishing world*
> *And round about I see the hosts of the dying,*
> *The young and the old; nor is there anywhere*
> *In all the world a refuge, or a harbor*
> *Where there is hope of safety. Funerals*
> *Where'er I turn my frightened eyes, appall;*
> *The temples groan with coffins, and the proud*
> *And the humble lie alike in lack of honor.*
> *The end of life presses upon my mind,*
> *And I recall the dear ones I have lost . . .*
> *The consecrated ground is all too small*
> *To hold the instant multitude of graves.*

1 Setting the Stage for the Black Death

The Middle Ages is the name commonly used for the era in European history lasting from the fall of the Roman Empire about A.D. 400 to the dawn of the great cultural revival known as the Renaissance about 1400. Traditionally, the Middle Ages is divided into three shorter periods: the early Middle Ages, lasting until the start of the eleventh century; the High Middle Ages, ending about 1250; and the late Middle Ages, which includes the Black Death pandemic of 1346–1352.

THE EARLY MIDDLE AGES: GREAT NOBLES AND IMPOVERISHED PEASANTS

The disintegration of the mighty Roman Empire in the fifth century A.D. threw Europe into chaos. Wracked by barbarian invasions and political instability, the continent's once thriving international trade all but disappeared, its cities declined, and most of its farmable land was divided into vast estates or manors, each ruled by a great noble or lord.

Throughout the early Middle Ages, the vast majority of Europeans were impoverished peasants, or serfs, who worked for one of the great landed nobles and lived on his manor.

11

Although they were not slaves who could be purchased or sold, serfs had few freedoms or rights. Typically, they and their descendants could not leave the manor, marry, or even sell an ox or sheep without first obtaining the lord's permission. Several days each week, the serfs toiled for free for their landlord, planting and harvesting his fields, caring for his livestock, cutting his firewood, and constructing and maintaining his buildings and fences. In addition to this arduous labor, masters burdened their tenants with a variety of taxes, which serfs usually paid off in the form of grain or other produce. Among other things, serfs were taxed for using their master's mill or winepress, marrying, having a child, or losing a spouse. In exchange for these fees and their labor on his manor, the lord provided his serfs with protection from outlaws and rival lords as well as a small strip of farmland for their personal use.

By the end of the early Middle Ages, a system of mutual obligations and services that would come to be called feudalism had taken firm root throughout much of Europe. Under feudalism, the handful of great nobles who controlled the land and dominated the economy also enjoyed enormous political, judicial, and military power. Within their own territories, lords could not only collect dues and taxes but also mint money, judge legal disputes, and defend their holdings and tenants with large personal armies of knights. Knights, members of the lesser nobility, were highly trained, mounted warriors who agreed to serve a lord in return for his pledge of protection and justice. Early medieval Europe was composed of a number of different kingdoms whose royal rulers were supposed to be the chief feudal lords of their realms. In practice, however, most European kings reigned supreme only within their own royal estates and had little influence over local lords or their knights and serfs.

THE HIGH MIDDLE AGES: PROSPERITY AND A POPULATION BOOM

During the High Middle Ages, Europe's population and economy exploded. The available food supply increased

During the early Middle Ages most Europeans were serfs, who labored in the fields of great nobles. In addition to working several days each week for their masters, serfs were also obliged to pay their lords a variety of taxes. In exchange, lords promised their serfs protection and a small plot of farmland for their personal use.

because of unusually mild weather conditions and advances in farming methods and technology. Better nutrition, combined with a long period of peace and the absence of any major disease epidemics, caused the continent's population to triple between 1000 and 1250, from approximately 25 million to 75 million. As the population swelled, new cities and towns sprang up, and trade flourished within Europe as well as with Asia and North Africa. The rise of commerce and towns encouraged the development of a new class of artisans, or skilled craftsmen, who fashioned shoes, cloth, and other goods to sell to their fellow townspeople and to the residents of the surrounding countryside.

Better food production techniques and an expanding economy brought new prosperity to the nobility, the burgeoning merchant and artisan classes, and even the lowest rung in European society—the peasants. After paying taxes and other fees to their lord and the Catholic Church, serfs usually managed to keep about half of the crops that they grew for themselves. Throughout the early Middle Ages, most peasants had barely enough grain and other produce left over to feed

The Catholic Church in the Middle Ages

The Catholic Church was not only the sole Christian church in medieval Europe, it was also the most powerful unifying structure on the continent. Aside from a small population of Jews, virtually everyone in Europe was a Catholic during the Middle Ages, and from birth to death, the church indelibly shaped their lives. All Christians were expected to attend Catholic services every week, to tithe—pay one-tenth of their income—to support the institution, and to strictly follow church laws and teachings. In return, they received the promise of a better afterlife in heaven than the short, brutal existence most of them were forced to endure on Earth.

The head of the Catholic Church, the pope, was the ultimate religious authority for all the Catholic clergy, including archbishops, bishops, priests, monks, and nuns, as well for the church's millions of lay (non-clergy) members. During their families, once their various obligations to their master and the church had been met. During the long, mild growing seasons of the High Middle Ages, however, many peasants were able to raise enough surplus grain and vegetables to sell to the inhabitants of Europe's booming cities and towns. The most enterprising serfs used these earnings to buy off some of their traditional work obligations to their lord, giving him cash in lieu of their labor. This, in turn, provided them with more time for their own agricultural pursuits. Many of these additional free hours were spent enlarging the manor's arable (cultivatable) land by draining marshes and clearing forests

most of the Middle Ages, popes also held enormous political sway over Europe's various kingdoms and their rulers. The pontiffs possessed a vital power: the ability to excommunicate anyone who defied the church. Excommunication meant that a person was forever barred from belonging to the church or attending its services. The threat of excommunication struck fear in the hearts of great monarchs and humble serfs alike since it was widely assumed that any Catholic who was ejected from the church was destined to spend eternity burning in hell.

At the center of every medieval town or manor was the local arm of the Catholic Church: the parish church. Its head, the parish priest, answered to a bishop—usually a noble— who oversaw groups of parishes called dioceses. Typically, parish priests were highly valued and influential members of their communities. In addition to conducting church services, they taught the Bible and Catholic doctrines to their flocks and ministered to the ill, the grieving, and the destitute.

and meadows on the fringes of their lord's estate. Most nobles allowed their laborers to till the newly cleared fields for themselves, although the serfs were still obliged to pay the lord rent for the privilege of using his land.

THE LATE MIDDLE AGES: OVERPOPULATION AND A STAGNANT FOOD SUPPLY

By the middle of the thirteenth century—the beginning of the period in medieval history known as the late Middle Ages—Europe's steadily expanding population was beginning to create serious problems on the continent. Virtually all of the farmable land in western Europe had already been cleared and planted. Some new land was still being brought under the plow, but it was generally swampy or rocky and poorly suited to agriculture. An ever-growing number of people, combined with a constant amount of workable land, meant that Europe's population was rapidly outstripping its available food supplies.

Today, Europe is home to more than 400 million persons. From the perspective of the early twenty-first century, it is hard to understand how mid-thirteenth-century Europe, with its 75 million inhabitants, could be viewed as anything but sparsely populated. Nonetheless, as John Kelly points out in his book *The Great Mortality: An Intimate History of the Black Death*, by the dawn of the late Middle Ages, "compared to the resources available to the population, the continent had become dangerously overcrowded."

Further widening the gap between the continent's stagnant food resources and swelling population was Europe's overdependence on wheat, which in the form of bread was a staple of the medieval diet. As Europe's population—and its demand for food—soared, more and more peasants focused their farming efforts on growing wheat. They realized that, of all the cereal grains commonly used to make bread, wheat produces the highest yields per seed planted. Moreover, they knew that they would be guaranteed a large market for their wheat crops since their contemporaries considered wheat as more nutritious and better tasting than other cereal grains such as rye, oats, and barley. Yet by devoting most of their fields to a single crop, the peasants were actually working against themselves. Monoculture (the growing of just one crop) rapidly exhausts soil, draining farmland of essential nutrients and making it less productive. Overreliance on a single food crop also meant that whenever the wheat crop failed because of disease or unfavorable weather conditions, widespread hunger was inevitable.

THE LITTLE ICE AGE AND THE GREAT FAMINE

By the late 1200s, the balance between Europe's agricultural resources and continually expanding population was becoming increasingly strained. Then something happened that no one could have predicted: Around the turn of the new century, the continent's climate took a turn for the worse. After decades of mild winters and springs and relatively dry summers, Europe entered what is sometimes referred to as the Little Ice Age, a period of bitterly cold winters and cool, unusually wet summers.

For a society as dependent on farming as medieval Europe was, deteriorating weather conditions spelled disaster. Waterlogged fields, stunted plants, and low crop yields had devastating consequences both for the continent's peasant masses and for its entire economy. As was true during the early Middle Ages, serfs again found themselves devoting virtually all their surplus crops to feeding their own families and paying off their debts to their lord and church. This left them with little or no money to spend on nonessential items, hurting artisans and merchants in nearby towns and cities. Because they were unable to raise their own grains or vegetables, all urban dwellers—not just merchants and artisans—suffered as one meager harvest followed another, and food prices skyrocketed. In England, the cost of wheat rose eightfold between 1313 and 1315, and in the city of Louvain in Flanders (modern Belgium), the market price of the increasingly scarce grain increased by more than 300 percent in just six months. Throughout Europe, living standards plummeted, and the continent became poorer and poorer.

By the early fourteenth century, a series of deadly famines had begun to sweep through Europe. In 1304 and 1305, thousands in northern France and the Netherlands died of starvation or from tuberculosis, pneumonia, or other contagious diseases that their hunger-weakened immune systems were incapable of fighting off. Then in 1309, following a summer of torrential downpours in which the wheat crop rotted in the fields and the hay used to feed livestock "lay so long under water that it could neither be mown nor gathered," according to one contemporary, Europe experienced its first continent-wide famine in more than two centuries. Although intermittent famines would afflict the continent right up until the outbreak of the Black Death in the mid-1340s, malnutrition and starvation were especially widespread between 1315 and 1322, a period in European history that has come to be known as the Great Famine.

During the seven years of the Great Famine, up to 20 percent of the population succumbed to starvation in some parts of Europe, with an estimated half-million people perishing in England alone. In Flanders, wrote an observer, "The cries that were heard from the poor would move a stone." High food costs drove desperate city dwellers to consume family pets, bird dung, and mildewed grain; in the countryside, peasants mortgaged their futures by butchering the oxen they relied on to plow their fields and devouring the seed grain needed for next year's planting. There were even rumors of people eating other people. According to one lurid account, at the height of the famine the Irish "were so destroyed by

The Black Death in the Middle East

While the Black Death was assaulting Europe during the late 1340s and early 1350s, the plague was also sweeping through the Middle East, which lost an estimated one-third of its population during the pandemic. The plague probably first arrived in the region from southern Russia. Among the western Asian and North African locales struck by the disease were the modern-day countries of Iran, Iraq, Egypt, Syria, Lebanon, Israel, Saudi Arabia, Yemen, and Turkey.

In late 1348, the Syrian geographer and devout Muslim Abu Hafs Umar ibn al-Wardi, who himself would die from the plague in March 1349, wrote a brief history of the pandemic. In his chronicle, he traces the path of the Black Death from Persia (modern-day Iran) to Egypt to Jerusalem and back northward through Lebanon and Syria to the city of Antioch in modern-day Turkey:

> The plague frightened and killed. . . . It attacked the Persians . . . and gnawed away at the Crimea. . . . It stilled all movement in Alexandria. . . .
>
> Then it attacked Gaza . . . [and] Jerusalem. . . . It then hastened its pace and attacked the entire maritime plain. The plague trapped Sidon and descended unexpectedly upon Beirut, cunningly. Next it directed the shooting of its arrows to Damascus. . . . To Antioch the plague gave its share. . . .
>
> How amazingly does it pursue the people of each house! One of them spits blood, and everyone in the household is certain of death. It brings the entire family to their graves after two or three nights. . . . Whoever tasted his own blood was sure to die.

hunger that they extracted bodies of the dead from cemeteries and dug out the flesh from their skulls and ate it." In Germany, a horrified monk reported, the poor even "devoured their own children."

WAR

During the course of the calamitous half century that preceded the coming of the Black Death in 1346, Europe was wracked not only by famine but also by war. On the Italian Peninsula, there was almost continuous fighting between the papacy and the German-led Holy Roman Empire for control of the Papal States; there was also discord between the rival trading centers of Venice and Genoa. Wars also raged in Spain, Germany, Scotland, and the duchies of Burgundy and Brittany, today provinces of France. (A duchy is territory ruled by a duke or duchess.)

The deadliest and largest conflict of the fourteenth century—and of the entire medieval era—was the Hundred Years' War between France and England, which was actually a series of intermittent battles that took place between 1337 and 1453. The chief cause of the war was a dispute between two ambitious and unusually powerful feudal kings, Edward II of England and Philip VI of France, over the status of English-held lands in what is today southwestern France.

The Hundred Years' War brought enormous misery to both England and France. Early in the war, the French repeatedly looted ports along England's western coast, disrupting the island kingdom's vital shipping trade and striking terror in the hearts of the towns' inhabitants. Since most of the battles of the Hundred Years' War were fought on French and not English soil, it was the people of France who suffered the most during the long conflict, however. Marauding English troops, many of them mercenaries (hired soldiers), went on a violent rampage through the French countryside, torching homes and farm fields, plundering livestock, raping women, and murdering countless innocent civilians. "Many people [have been] slaughtered, churches pillaged, . . . maids and virgins deflowered, respectable wives and widows dishonored, town, manor, and buildings burnt," lamented one French observer.

The Battle of Crecy (1346) is depicted in the fifteenth-century illustration (above). The Hundred Years' War between England and France took a psychological and physical toll on both the English and French population during the Middle Ages, possibly making them more susceptible to contracting illness and less successful in fighting it off.

Historians can only speculate regarding the relationship between the destructive wars and other calamities that afflicted late medieval Europe and the Black Death pandemic of 1346–1352. Still, many historians believe that the intermittent famines, severe weather, and violent conflicts that beset the continent during the first half of the 1300s took a toll on inhabitants' overall health, making them more likely to contract—and die from—infectious diseases such as the plague. Whether or not these scholars are correct, at least this much can be said with certainty: On the eve of the greatest pandemic to ever hit the continent, European society was already reeling from a series of devastating crises, both natural and manmade.

2 What Was the Black Death?

Ever since the late 1800s when researchers first began to unlock the secrets of the gruesome disease, most historians and scientists have assumed that bubonic plague was the chief agent of the Black Death. Bubonic plague is marked by a variety of symptoms, including headache, fever, chills, rapid pulse rate, extreme thirst, mental confusion, muscle aches, vomiting, diarrhea, and exhaustion. The disease's most recognizable symptom, however, is the bubo—a tender, egg-shaped bulge that usually develops on or near the infected person's inner thighs, armpits, or neck. The painful swellings that gave bubonic plague its name result from the buildup of dead cells and disease-carrying germs in the lymph nodes, small masses of tissue in the body where such impurities collect. If left untreated, bubonic plague typically kills three out of five of its victims within two weeks. Its two close relations, pneumonic plague and septicemic plague, are even more lethal. If untreated, the death rate for these less common variants of the plague is nearly 100 percent.

The telltale symptom of bubonic plague was buboes, or lumps in the underarm and groin area caused by swollen lymph nodes. The egg-shaped bulges that gave bubonic plague its name are the result of an accumulation of dead cells and bacteria in the lymph nodes, glandlike masses of tissue where such impurities accumulate.

A NINETEENTH-CENTURY MEDICAL REVOLUTION

When the Great Mortality swept through Europe during the mid-1300s and for hundreds of years after the pandemic, physicians and scientists could only guess at what lay behind the deadly outbreak. Most blamed the Black Death—and disease in general—either on an imbalance of fluids in the body or on poisonous vapors in the air. As late as the 1830s, a leading German physician named J.F. Hecker published a book on the Great Mortality in which he hypothesized that poisonous gases released into the atmosphere by a series of small earthquakes had caused the pandemic.

About a half century after the publication of Hecker's book, two researchers, the French biologist Louis Pasteur and the German physician Robert Koch, developed a revolutionary new theory regarding the origins of disease. According to Pasteur and Koch's startling hypothesis, illness results when microorganisms—creatures too tiny to be seen with the naked eye—invade the body. Two major types of disease-causing microorganisms—or germs, as they are commonly known—are bacteria and viruses. Eventually, scientists were able to determine that certain strains of bacteria produce such common infections as strep throat and pneumonia, while specific strains of viruses cause measles, influenza, chicken pox, and other widespread illnesses.

Although the established medical community was at first skeptical of Pasteur and Koch's new ideas regarding disease, the two researchers quickly attracted enthusiastic students to their laboratories. Two of the most gifted of these young scientists were Alexandre Yersin, a Swiss-born biologist who studied under Pasteur in Paris, and Shibasaburo Kitasato, a Japanese-born biologist who studied with Koch in Berlin. During the 1890s, after Yersin and Kitasato had completed their training with Pasteur and Koch and launched their own research careers, the bubonic plague struck East Asia with a vengeance, marking the first major outbreak of the disease anywhere in the world in more than a century. Inspired by their mentors' teachings about disease and germs, both Yersin and Kitasato vowed to uncover the microorganism behind Asia's terrible new pandemic.

UNRAVELING THE MYSTERIES OF THE BUBONIC PLAGUE

In early 1894, Yersin and Kitasato set out separately for the British colony of Hong Kong in the South China Sea to study the plague firsthand. In recent years, Kitasato had become famous within the scientific community for his groundbreaking work on the deadly disease tetanus. Deeply impressed by the Japanese biologist's international reputation and the large entourage of assistants he brought along with him to the colony, Hong Kong's administrators offered Kitasato a well-equipped laboratory in the island's finest hospital. They also allowed him full access to the hospital

After studying under famed scientist Louis Pasteur, Alexandre Yersin *(above)* traveled to Hong Kong to find the strain of plague that was spreading throughout Asia and Europe. Despite his lack of sophisticated equipment and access to samples, Yersin managed to isolate and identify the bacterium that caused bubonic plague.

morgue so that he could examine the cadavers of plague patients. In contrast, when Yersin, a relative unknown in the world of research, arrived in Hong Kong without a single assistant in tow, the British authorities scorned the young scientist. Yersin was forced to conduct his investigations in a crude bamboo hut that he helped build. Refused access to local morgues, Yersin turned to bribery to obtain material for his research, paying British soldiers to let him dissect the bodies of impoverished plague victims before the corpses were dumped into mass graves.

Yersin was not one to give up easily, however. He put in long days in his makeshift laboratory and by the summer of 1894 had achieved a major breakthrough in pinning down the plague's origins. By meticulously examining pus samples from the buboes of corpses under his microscope, Yersin was able to isolate and identify a previously unknown bacterium (the singular form for bacteria). While Kitasato focused his attention on dissected cadaver organs and on what would turn out to be a harmless microorganism in the blood, Yersin zeroed in on the real culprit: a rod-shaped bacterium, or bacillus, that he named *Pasteurella pestis* in honor of his teacher, Louis Pasteur. (*Pestis* is short for pestilence, meaning a deadly epidemic disease.) Many years later, the bacillus would be renamed *Yersinia pestis*, usually shortened to *Y. pestis*, in recognition of its discoverer.

THE PATH OF *Y. PESTIS*: FROM RATS TO FLEAS TO HUMANS

Now researchers turned to the question of how *Y. pestis* found its way into the human population. From the start, Yersin was convinced that the plague bacillus, like many other types of infectious germs, was transmitted to people by rodent and insect vectors, or carriers. Soon two other scientists, Paul-Louis Simond of France and Masanori Ogata of Japan, confirmed Yersin's hypothesis. Simond's and Ogata's research in plague-ridden India and China directly connected *Y. pestis* to two nonhuman carriers: a species of rat that likes to live close to humans—the black, or house, rat; *Rattus rattus (R. rattus)*—and a species of flea that preys on *R. rattus* and humans alike—the oriental rat flea; *Xenopsylla cheopis (X. cheopis).*

Shortly after Simond and Ogata tied *R. rattus* and *X. cheopis* to the pandemic surging across Asia, scientists achieved another crucial step in revealing the mysteries of the bubonic plague. They determined how the rat flea contracts *Y. pestis*

The Plague of Justinian

The first bubonic plague pandemic to strike Europe probably occurred some 700–800 years before the Black Death, during the sixth and seventh centuries A.D. The pandemic appears to have erupted around 541, when Emperor Justinian I ruled the East Roman, or Byzantine, Empire, and is therefore usually referred to as the Plague of Justinian. Most contemporaries described the outbreak as beginning in Egypt and then spreading by sea to Justinian's capital city of Constantinople (now Istanbul, Turkey), the Middle East, the Italian Peninsula, and the southern coast of France.

Although few eyewitness descriptions of the pandemic have survived, most historians agree that the disease that raged through western and southern Europe, western Asia, and North Africa during the sixth and seventh centuries was bubonic plague. The historical sources frequently refer to boils and bulges on the infected persons' bodies that sound very from the black rat in the first place, then passes the dangerous germ on to people.

Like all fleas, *X. cheopis* is a parasite, meaning that it lives off other organisms, called hosts. The flea's primary food source is its host's blood, and the tiny insect's mouth parts are well designed for piercing the skin of animals and humans. Although the oriental rat flea will attack many different species of rodents and other mammals, its host of choice is *R. rattus*. At any given time, dozens—even hundreds—of *X. cheopis* may live in the fur of a single, diseased black

much like buboes. In Constantinople during the 540s, the court chronicler, Procopios, described the stricken as suffering not only from painful boils but also from mental confusion, another common symptom of the bubonic plague. A few decades later, as the pandemic continued to devastate the Byzantine Empire, a lawyer in the city of Antioch noted that victims endured high fevers, diarrhea, and tender swellings—all symptoms of the bubonic plague.

Modern historians can only speculate regarding how many people died during the Plague of Justinian, but according to contemporary observers, the mortality rate was shockingly high. When communities ran out of coffins, the dead were simply thrown into mass graves, one eyewitness reported. Procopios claimed that fully half of the population of Constantinople perished as a result of the pandemic, while in hard-hit rural areas, so many people died that crops and livestock were reportedly left untended.

rat and feast off its blood. After ingesting the sick rodent's blood, the insect parasites rapidly become infected with *Y. pestis* as well.

Once inside *X. cheopis*, the plague germs begin to multiply wildly. The rapidly growing bacteria lodge in the flea's digestive tract, preventing the insect from absorbing any nutrients from the rat blood it ingests. This, in turn, makes the flea voraciously hungry. Yet by this time *X. cheopis*'s rat host has typically succumbed to the plague. Desperate for a new source of blood, the insects flee their lifeless rodent hosts for a new food source—very often *R. rattus*'s close neighbor—humans. In a healthy *X. cheopis*, blood sucked from the rat host flows straight into the flea's stomach. In an insect infected with *Y. pestis*, however, the multiplying bacteria create a blockage in the flea's foregut, or upper stomach. Consequently, when *X. cheopis* bites its new human host, the sick flea gags and vomits undigested, bacteria-tainted rat blood directly into the open skin wound: a revolting but highly efficient means of spreading the plague bacillus. Adding to its effectiveness as a plague transmitter is the fact that *X. cheopis* can survive for at least six weeks without a host, if necessary. During the Middle Ages, six weeks would have given the wingless insect plenty of time to journey hundreds of miles to new human communities in shipments of wheat or cloth.

THE BUBONIC PLAGUE AND THE BLACK DEATH ARE LINKED

It did not take long for Alexandre Yersin and the other researchers who observed the bubonic plague firsthand during the Asian pandemic to come to the conclusion that the famous Great Mortality of the Middle Ages was the same disease then ravaging China and India. Indeed, the evidence that the pandemic that terrorized Europe 500 years earlier was plague was very persuasive.

As Yersin and his colleagues who personally witnessed the horrors of the Asian pandemic of the late nineteenth century knew only too well, the most distinctive symptom of bubonic

A Contemporary Description of the Black Death by Giovanni Boccaccio

In his famous collection of stories, *The Decameron*, the fourteenth-century Italian writer Giovanni Boccaccio (1313?–1375) vividly depicts the symptoms of the Black Death, which swept through his native city of Florence during the spring and summer of 1348. In his account, Boccaccio refers to egg- and apple-shaped swellings that the people of Florence called *gavoccioli*. Most historians assume that Boccaccio was describing the characteristic buboes of plague victims:

> Its [the plague's] earliest symptom, in men and women alike, was the appearance of certain swellings in the groin or the armpit, some of which were egg-shaped whilst others were roughly the size of the common apple. Sometimes the swellings were large, sometimes not so large, and they were referred to by the populace as *gavoccioli*. From the two areas already mentioned, this deadly *gavoccioli* would begin to spread, and within a short time it would appear at random all over the body. . . . Few of those who caught [the illness] ever recovered, and in most cases death occurred within three days from the appearance of the symptoms we have described, some people dying more rapidly than others. . . .

plague are buboes—the agonizing welts and bulges that usually develop on or near a sufferer's inner thighs, neck, or armpits. These ugly swellings are formed when the swiftly multiplying *Y. pestis* bacteria, having overwhelmed the body's ability to fight off the infection, build up in the victim's lymph nodes. During the Black Death, contemporary accounts of the pandemic are filled with descriptions of the "boils," "lumps," and "ulcers" that tormented the sick: "Boils developed in different parts of the body, . . . on the thighs, or on the arms, and in others on the neck. At first these were the size of a hazelnut . . . . Soon the boils grew to the size of a walnut, then to that of a hen's egg or a goose's egg, and they were exceedingly painful . . . ," wrote an Italian observer. "Lumps suddenly erupted in their armpits or groin," a French friar reported several years later, "and their appearance was an infallible sign of death." Across the English Channel in the pestilence-stricken town of Reading, another monk lamented that painful "ulcers . . . tortured the dying for three days."

When Simond and Ogata tied the bacillus that Alexandre Yersin had isolated to *R. rattus* and then to *X. cheopis*, the connection between the bubonic plague and the Great Mortality became even clearer to scientists and historians alike. In common with much of the Chinese and Indian population during the late 1800s, most people in the Middle Ages lived in primitive, unsanitary conditions—the perfect breeding ground for plague-carrying rats and fleas. Garbage, sewage, and the blood of slaughtered livestock filled the streets of medieval towns, attracting armies of hungry black rats, and the dirt floors and porous wattle and daub (twig and mud) walls and thatched roofs of the typical fourteenth-century house made appealing homes for the bacteria-laden rodents. Moreover, scholars noted, like many plague victims in the Asian pandemic, medieval people usually lived close to their farm animals, exposing them further to diseased fleas and rats. Finally, personal hygiene was poor among the impoverished masses hardest hit by the nineteenth-century pandemic, just as it was among the inhabitants of medieval Europe, who generally viewed bathing as unnecessary and even unhealthy and rarely washed their bodies, clothes, or bedding. The poor personal hygiene habits of most medieval Europeans— including even the well-off—not only served to attract more fleas but also helped to ensure the survival of the tiny plague vectors in the belongings and on the bodies of their human hosts, scientists and historians reasoned.

PNEUMONIC AND SEPTICEMIC PLAGUE

Today, most scholars agree that the evidence tying the bubonic plague to the Black Death is convincing. Nonetheless, not long after the medieval pandemic and the deadly illness caused by *Y. pestis* were first linked, researchers began to note that some medieval accounts of the Great Mortality did not mesh with bubonic plague's usual symptoms. This, in turn, led scientists to identify two relatively uncommon but highly lethal variants of the plague: pneumonic and septicemic plague.

According to medieval eyewitnesses, not all of the Great Mortality's victims developed the painful swellings that are the bubonic plague's most characteristic symptom. Many scholars now believe that a small percentage of these individuals may have contracted a very rare form of the plague known as septicemic plague, which occurs when the *Y. pestis* bacillus directly invades the bloodstream. In the days before the development of antibiotics to combat bacterial infections in the 1940s, the death rate for this extraordinarily virulent type of plague was essentially 100 percent. Death from untreated septicemic plague is not only virtually inescapable but also shockingly sudden. It usually occurs within just 14 hours of the onset of symptoms as the bacteria rapidly overwhelm the circulatory system, causing severe damage to the heart and other vital organs and widespread hemorrhaging (profuse bleeding from ruptured blood vessels). When chroniclers of the Black Death wrote of sick persons literally dropping dead on the streets or going to bed apparently healthy and dying the

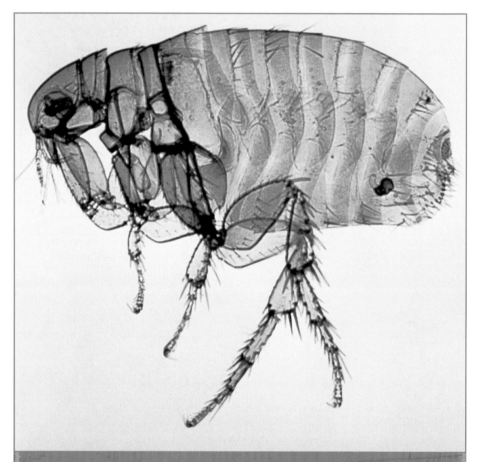

The connection between diseased rats and sick humans is the oriental rat flea *(above)*, a blood-sucking insect smaller than the head of a pin. After their furry hosts succumbed to bubonic plague, these voracious fleas would move on to humans, infecting and killing an estimated 25–45 million people during the Middle Ages.

following morning, they may very well have been describing victims of septicemic plague.

A second highly lethal variant of the plague that many scholars believe played a far more important role in the Black Death than septicemic plague is pneumonic—or pulmonary—plague, in which the *Y. pestis* bacillus invades the lungs. In common with septicemic plague, before antibiotic drugs were developed in the mid-twentieth century pneumonic plague generally killed so swiftly that patients did not have time to develop the telltale buboes of the diseases' cousin, bubonic plague. The principal signs of pneumonic plague are a hacking cough and the spitting up of blood, and for 95 to 100 percent of untreated sufferers, death occurs within one to three days of the onset of symptoms. Unlike other forms of the plague, pneumonic plague can be transmitted directly from one person to another when the infected individual coughs or sneezes.

Today, pneumonic plague is relatively rare, making up between 5 to 15 percent of plague cases worldwide. But the disease seems to have been considerably more prevalent during the Black Death pandemic. Numerous medieval sources describe stricken persons gasping for breath and "vomiting" blood, noting that coughing up bloody sputum was an almost infallible sign that death was near. "Breath," wrote one horrified chronicler of the Great Mortality, "spread the infection among those speaking together . . . and it seemed as if the victim[s] were struck all at once by the affliction and shattered by it. . . . Victims violently coughed up blood, and after three days of incessant vomiting for which there was no remedy, they died, and with them died not only everyone who talked with them but also anyone who had acquired or touched or laid hands on their belongings."

The victims of the lethal pandemic that ravaged Europe from 1346 until 1352 were totally in the dark regarding the true biological origins of their suffering. Today, however, most scholars concur that the bacterial infection known as bubonic plague, and to a lesser degree its highly deadly variants, pneumonic and septicemic plague, were the chief agents of the Black Death.

The Path of the Black Death

The exact point of origin of the Black Death has been a matter of debate among historians and scientists for years. Among the places that have been suggested by scholars over the centuries are China, India, and southern Russia. The most recent research, however, points to the remote steppes, or arid grasslands, of central Asia as the source of the disastrous pandemic. Located to the east of the Caspian Sea, a large saltwater lake that separates southeastern Europe from southwestern Asia, the central Asiatic steppes extend through the present-day countries of Turkmenistan, Uzbekistan, Kazakhstan, and Kyrgyzstan.

THE STEPPES OF CENTRAL ASIA: A VAST PLAGUE RESERVOIR

Scientists have identified the vast grasslands of central Asia as one of the world's major plague reservoirs. That means that *Y. pestis*, the bacillus that causes bubonic, pneumonic, and septicemic plague, occurs naturally within the region's large wild rodent population, including among the tarabagan. The tarabagan is a burrowing, squirrel-like rodent that happens to

be a favorite host of the plague-carrying oriental rat flea, or
X. cheopis. Although it has become a relatively rare disease in
modern times, even today people occasionally catch bubonic
plague in the central Asiatic steppes.

Assuming that central Asia was indeed the cradle of the
pandemic that devastated medieval Europe, just when and
how the plague leapt from the local rodent population and
their flea parasites to the region's human population remains
a mystery. Although there were occasional flare-ups of the disease in East Asia over the centuries, Asia and Europe had been
spared major outbreaks of bubonic plague since the 500s, when
the Plague of Justinian swept through the Middle East and
the Mediterranean area. Scholars speculate that a significant
environmental disturbance—possibly an earthquake or severe
drought—occurred during the early 1300s that destroyed
rodent food supplies. In the wake of this natural calamity, scientists believe, hordes of *Y. pestis*–carrying rodents fled their
traditional habitat and migrated toward central Asia's human
communities, where food—and colonies of black or house rats
(*R. rattus*) ripe for infection—was plentiful.

To date, several ancient gravestones are the only archaeo-
logical evidence linking the bubonic plague with the steppe's
human inhabitants during the years leading up to the Black
Death. Archaeologists discovered the simple stone markers near Issyk Kul Lake in present-day Kyrgyzstan, close to
a known plague reservoir. Like numerous other medieval
headstones in the area, the gravestones are inscribed with
the dates 1338 and 1339. Clearly, some catastrophe must have
struck Issyk Kul during those years, less than a decade before
the Black Death appeared in Europe. According to the three
gravestones from 1338 and 1339 that provide a cause of death,
that catastrophe was a severe and highly contagious disease, an
illness that many historians assume was the bubonic plague.
"This is the grave of Kutluk," reads one of the markers. "He

died of the plague [also translated as "pestilence"] with his wife Magnu-Kelka."

THE PLAGUE MOVES OUT OF CENTRAL ASIA

By the late 1330s and early 1340s, the pandemic that would later come to be known as the Black Death had begun to trickle out of central Asia, scholars believe. It seems to have headed eastward toward China first, probably by means of the Silk Road, the famous network of trade routes that once linked

Bubonic plague is believed to have originated in Central Asia, a region where the bacterium for the illness is thought to occur naturally in the rodents who inhabit the area. After migrating east, these rodents and their fleas passed the plague to the black rat *(above)*, whose close proximity to people resulted in human infections.

the Mediterranean region and central Asia to the Far East. From China, the plague appears to have moved southward and westward on merchant vessels to India. Bacteria-carrying black rats were able to transport the plague for hundreds of miles by stowing away on merchant ships, which the rodents did in such large numbers during the Middle Ages that they were given the nickname of "ship rats." The oriental rat fleas that pass the *Y. pestis* bacillus directly to humans through bites were also capable of conveying the plague over vast distances. Able to survive for six weeks without a host, the tiny parasites are thought to have traveled hundreds of miles in cloth, grain, and other trade items commonly carried on medieval ships and overland caravans.

By the mid-1340s, the plague was journeying westward as well as eastward out of the steppes, moving relentlessly toward the Middle East and southeastern Europe by land and sea. Once again, merchants—and the infected rats and fleas that they unwittingly carried with them—were probably the chief transporters of the plague from its central Asian point of origin. In the case of the bubonic plague's highly lethal relation, the pneumonic plague, infected traders traveling by overland routes could transmit the disease directly to people they encountered on the way, who in turn spread the illness to their own families and communities.

In 1346, a reliable Russian source placed the plague on the western side of the Caspian Sea. According to the eyewitness, the deadly disease attacked several cities and towns bordering the large saltwater lake, including Sarai, near the modern-day Russian city of Volgograd. Sarai was not only a busy trading center but also the capital city of the Golden Horde, a Mongol group who ruled Russia for more than two centuries during the Middle Ages. Natives of the central Asiatic steppes, the Mongols were exceptionally accomplished horsemen and warriors. Under the leadership of the famous Genghis (or

Chingis) Khan, they founded a vast transcontinental empire during the thirteenth century. By the end of the 1200s, Mongol territories stretched all the way from China in the east to Hungary in the west. As it turned out, Russia's Mongol occupiers were to play a vital role in bringing the Black Death into the heart of Europe.

THE MONGOLS AND THE PLAGUE

Just three years before the plague reached Sarai, the Mongol army began a siege of the Italian-controlled Black Sea port of Kaffa (also spelled Caffa) on the Crimean Peninsula. Technically, the Golden Horde ruled all of the Crimea, including Kaffa, today the Ukrainian city of Feodosiya. Nonetheless, eager to encourage trade within their far-flung empire, the Mongols permitted merchants from the great Italian commercial center of Genoa to take charge of the busy port city.

Relations between the Genoese traders and their Mongol hosts were frequently strained, chiefly because of religious differences: The Italians were staunch Catholics, whereas the Mongols had enthusiastically adopted the Islamic faith during the 1200s. In 1343, decades of Genoese-Mongol tension in southern Russia finally erupted into violence. Several Italian merchants got into a bloody brawl with local Muslims in the Crimean town of Tana, and one Muslim was killed. Determined to defend the honor of Islam, the Mongols threatened to execute the slain Muslim's Christian assailants. With the Mongol army in hot pursuit, the terrified merchants fled Tana for nearby Kaffa. To the traders' enormous relief, the city's Italian-Catholic authorities immediately offered the men refuge behind Kaffa's high walls. Arriving at Kaffa's gates a short while later, the Mongols discovered that the Genoese had locked them out. Enraged by the Italians' audacity, the Mongols vowed to force the Genoese into submission by laying siege to the walled city.

By the end of 1346, the pestilence that had already devastated Sarai reached Kaffa's Mongol besiegers, who had massed directly outside the city's walls. According to a contemporary account of the siege by an Italian notary (legal scribe), Gabriel de Mussis, the stricken soldiers quickly discovered that "all medical advice and attention was useless. The Tartars [Mongols] died as soon as the signs of disease appeared on their bodies: swellings in the armpit or groin caused by coagulating

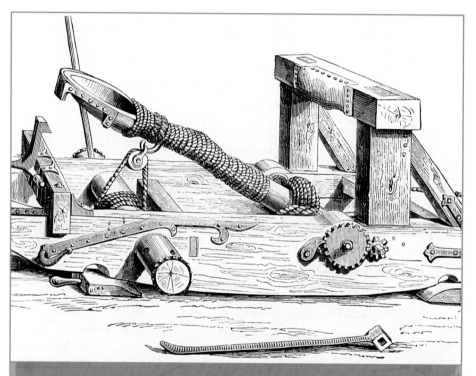

The plague was so deadly that it even was used as a military tactic. While besieging the walled city of Kaffa on the Black Sea, the Mongol army was stricken with the bubonic plague. As soldier after soldier fell, the Mongols began to use a catapult *(above)* to fling corpses over the protective walls, hoping to infect Kaffa's population, weaken the city's defenses, and invade.

humors [thickening bodily fluids], followed by a putrid fever." So many of the besiegers died that the survivors, utterly over-whelmed by the number of corpses in need of burial, began stacking dead bodies like firewood against the thick walls that surrounded Kaffa.

Then the Mongols came up with an ingenious—and gruesome—plan. If they loaded the infected corpses onto catapults and hurled them over the city walls at the Italians, perhaps Kaffa's defenders would also fall ill and die, they reasoned. According to de Mussis, the Golden Horde's early experiment with biological warfare was highly effective. "What seemed like mountains of dead were thrown into the city," reported de Mussis. "And the Christians could not hide or flee or escape from them, although they dumped as many of the bodies as they could in the sea. And soon the rotting corpses tainted the air . . . [and] poisoned the water supply, and the stench was so overwhelming that hardly one man in several thousand was in a position to flee the remains of the Tartar army. No one knew, or could discover, a means of defense."

Many modern scholars insist that de Mussis's version of how the plague spread to the Italian defenders of Kaffa is untenable, arguing that the disease cannot be caught merely through contact with infected corpses. They believe that the illness probably made its way into Kaffa when *Y. pestis*–bearing rats slipped through cracks in the city's walls. According to microbiologist Mark Wheelis in his article "Biological Warfare at the 1346 Siege of Caffa," however, de Mussis's account of how the plague traveled from the Mongol encampment into the Italian-held city is entirely plausible. The Golden Horde's gory strategy of launching *Y. pestis*–infected cadavers over Kaffa's walls could "easily have transmitted the plague" to those unfor-tunate Genoese who were allotted the task of disposing of the mangled bodies, noted Wheelis:

Contact with infected material [from a bubo] is a known mechanism of transmission; for instance, among 284 cases of plague in the United States in 1970–1995 for which a mechanism of transmission could be reasonably inferred, 20 percent were thought to be by direct contact. Such transmission would have been especially likely at Caffa, where cadavers would have been badly mangled by being hurled, and many of the defenders probably had cut or abraded [scraped] hands from coping with the bombardment.

TO THE MEDITERRANEAN SEA

Desperate to get out of the plague-stricken city, sometime during the late summer or early autumn of 1347, the Genoese finally gave up their stubborn stand against the Mongols and fled Kaffa on their trading ships. Their destination was the Mediterranean Sea and their Italian homeland. Yet with the unwitting Genoese merchants traveled the horrific disease they sought to escape.

In October 1347, 12 Genoese galleys drifted into the harbor of Messina, Sicily, just off the southern tip of the Italian Peninsula. Just how many of the ships' passengers and crews had fallen sick and died before reaching the Mediterranean island is unknown. Yet there can be no doubt that the lethal *Y. pestis* bacillus was on board. According to eyewitnesses, about a week or so after the vessels docked, the people of Messina began to develop the characteristic swellings and high fever of the bubonic plague. As rats and fleas from the ships spread the microorganism to the port's rodent colonies and human inhabitants and more and more Messinians died, the survivors panicked. Hundreds fled their native town for other parts of Sicily, taking the disease with them wherever they went.

Within months, the Black Death had reached a number of major port cities on the Italian mainland, including Genoa, Venice, and Pisa, probably having been transported there by merchant ships from infected Crimean and Middle Eastern ports. By the winter of 1348, the plague was in the beautiful and cosmopolitan city of Florence, where it killed an

Messina Confronts the Plague

Sometime in late 1347, the Black Death struck the port city of Messina in northeastern Sicily, a large island in the Mediterranean Sea off the coast of southern Italy. According to eyewitness Michael da Piazza, a member of the Roman Catholic religious order the Franciscans, the people of Messina were utterly terrified by the mysterious and rapidly spreading illness, which they believed could be contracted from even the slightest exposure to the stricken:

> Soon men hated each other so much that, if a son was attacked by the disease, his father would not care for him. . . . As the number of deaths increased in Messina, many wished to confess their sins to the priests and to draw up their last will and testament. But ecclesiastics [clergymen], lawyers and attorneys refused to enter the houses of the diseased. . . .
>
> Soon the corpses were lying forsaken in the houses. No ecclesiastic, no son, no father and no relation dared to enter, but they paid servants high wages to bury the dead. The houses of the deceased remained open, with all their valuables, with gold and jewels; anyone who decided to enter met with no impediment, for the plague raged with such vehemence that soon there was a shortage of servants and finally none were left at all.

estimated 60,000 people, about half the city's population. In his famous book, *The Decameron*, Florentine native Giovanni Boccaccio described the terrible toll that *Y. pestis* took on his beloved hometown: "Many died by day or by night in the public streets: the departure of many others, who died at home, was hardly observed by their neighbors until the stench of their putrefying bodies carried the tidings; and what with their corpses and the corpses of others who died on every hand the whole place was a sepulchre [burial vault]."

THE BLACK DEATH SWEEPS THROUGH WESTERN AND CENTRAL EUROPE

About the same time that the Great Mortality was assaulting Florence, the plague was also hammering Marseille, a bustling

A Nursery Rhyme and the Black Death

> Ring-a-ring a rosie,
> A pocket full of posies,
> A-tishoo, a-tishoo,
> All fall down.
> Ring around the rosie,
> A pocket full of posies,
> Ashes, ashes,
> All fall down.

During the mid-twentieth century, some people began to suggest that the popular folk rhyme "Ring Around the Rosie" dated back to the Black Death era in England and was, in fact,

French port on the Mediterranean Sea. From this major commercial hub, the disease fanned out in all directions, spreading southward into Spain and westward and northward through France. By the summer of 1348, the pandemic had reached Paris, where it raged on for months. "The multitude of people who died . . . was so great that nothing like it was ever heard, read of, or witnessed in past ages," one French commentator noted in awe. In some parts of the city, he claimed, "two did not remain alive out of every twenty."

During the second half of 1348, the Black Death all but engulfed western and central Europe, traveling "with the speed of a fire racing through dry or oil substances that happened to be placed within its reach," wrote Boccaccio in his introduction to *The Decameron*. Moving out of northeastern

inspired by the lethal pandemic. The word *rosie*, the theory's supporters claimed, referred to a rash that some plague victims developed, while the phrase *pocket full of posies* referred to the flower petals that people often carried around with them during the pandemic because the fragrant blossoms were thought to ward off illness. "Ashes, ashes" was said to refer to the cremation, or burning, of infected corpses (although most plague victims seem to have been buried in mass graves), and the phrase *all fall down* to the fact that most people who contracted the sickness died from it. Some scholars, however, remain unconvinced by the supposed relationship between the popular children's rhyme and the Black Death. They contend that there is no absolutely evidence that the rhyme dates as far back as the 1300s, pointing out that "Ring Around the Rosie" did not even appear in print until 1881.

Italy, it traversed the Alps, entering Switzerland, Austria, and southern Germany. In central Europe, Hungary was hit hard. From the trading centers of northern and western France, the plague made its way to Flanders (modern Belgium) and the Netherlands and crossed the English Channel, attacking Britain with a vengeance. By the end of 1349, Ireland had also been invaded by what one British priest dubbed the "dreadful pestilence," and London had lost an estimated 20,000 people, or 40 percent of the city's total population.

NORTHERN AND EASTERN EUROPE ARE STRICKEN

The year 1349 saw the Great Mortality move into Scandinavia, first attacking Denmark, which had an extensive sea trade with England, then menacing Sweden, Norway, and Iceland. The plague also invaded Scotland in 1349, probably brought northward from England by Scottish soldiers. The following year, the Black Death made its way all the way northward to the Arctic Circle via Scandinavian supply ships, where it wiped out entire Icelandic and Norwegian colonies on the remote island of Greenland. In 1350, the plague also visited eastern Europe for the first time. The devastation that the disease wrought there was not as widespread as in other parts of the continent, perhaps because eastern Europe was sparsely settled and had few outside trading contacts. Significant portions of Poland and Bohemia (which roughly corresponds to today's Czech Republic) seem to have been spared altogether. In late 1351, the pestilence finally reached northwestern Russia for the first time, invading Moscow sometime in 1352.

By the time it entered Moscow in 1352, the pandemic had run its course throughout most of the rest of Europe. By the end of the year, it had petered out altogether on the continent. Historians can only guess how many people perished during the Great Mortality. Most modern scholars place mortality rates for the Black Death anywhere from 33 percent to a staggering 60 percent of Europe's population—an estimated 25 million to 45 million persons. Bewildered and terrified by the deadly scourge, Europeans struggled to come to terms with what has been described as the worst natural disaster in the continent's history.

4 The Black Death Psyche

The Black Death had an enormous impact on the psychological as well as the physical well-being of the communities it ravaged. As people struggled to come to terms with a cruel and mysterious killer against which they were utterly powerless, they were often overwhelmed by feelings of grief, hopelessness, guilt, anger, or fear. In contemporary accounts of the Great Mortality, wrote Susan Scott and Christopher Duncan in *The Return of the Black Death: The World's Greatest Serial Killer,* "We read repeatedly that parents even left their dying children untended, something that we find almost unimaginable. But we have never come face to face with anything like the full horror of the Black Death, an apparently wildly infectious disease that struck from out of nowhere. There was no cure, no way of alleviating the agony, no clean hospitals in which to die peacefully, no painkillers, absolutely nothing anyone could do."

THE SCOPE OF THE TRAGEDY: "THE DEAD WERE NUMBERLESS"

Eyewitness descriptions of the pandemic provide insight not only into the scope of the tragedy but also the enormous psychological and emotional toll it exacted from the people of Europe. "Sorrow is on all sides; fear is everywhere," wrote the great medieval poet, Petrarch (1304–1374), in a letter to his brother regarding his sojourn in the plague-stricken city of Parma in northern Italy:

> I wish, my brother, that I had never been born, or at least had died before these times. . . . When has any such thing ever been heard or seen; in what annals has it ever been read that houses were left vacant, cities deserted, the country neglected, the fields too small for the dead to be buried, and a fearful and universal solitude over the whole earth?
>
> Will posterity ever believe these things when we, who see them, can scarcely credit them? We would think we were dreaming if we did not, with our own eyes, when we walk abroad, see the city in mourning with funerals, and on returning home, find it empty, and thus know that what we lament is real.

In *Cronaca Senese*, an account of the Black Death in Siena, Italy, Agnolo di Tura, the father of five young children, vividly describes his own highly personal encounter with the Great Mortality and the profound sense of hopelessness that pervaded his hometown:

> In many places in Siena great pits were dug and piled deep with the multitude of dead. And they died by the hundreds, both day and night, and all were thrown in those ditches and covered with earth. And as soon as those ditches were filled, more were dug. And I, Agnolo di Tura, called the Fat, buried my five children with my own hands. And there were also those who were so sparsely covered with earth that the dogs dragged them forth and devoured many bodies throughout the city. There was no

one who wept for any death, for all awaited death. And so many died that all believed it was the end of the world.

Another Italian chronicler of the plague, Gabriel de Mussis, also conveys something of the desperation and panic that afflicted entire European communities during the Black Death. In his *Historia de Morbo* (History of the Death), he recalled how in his native city of Piacenza "the dead were numberless." De Mussis reported: "So great was the mortality that men hardly dared to breathe." He went on to present a chilling account of plague-stricken boys and girls locked out of their own homes by their terrified parents. According to de Mussis, the betrayed children would plant themselves on their parents' doorsteps and beg to be allowed in: "'Oh father, why have you abandoned me? Do you forget that I am your child? Oh mother, . . . why are you now so cruel to me when only yesterday you were so kind?'" the young plague victims would call out tearfully.

Hundreds of miles away from the Italian Peninsula in Great Britain, a monk named William of Dene witnessed the Black Death's lethal assault on his home county of Kent. The *Rochester Chronicle*, William's grim account of the pandemic in southeastern England, echoes the Italians' portrayals of a society engulfed by suffering and death. "The mortality swept away so vast a multitude of both sexes that none could be found to carry the corpses to the grave," the monk lamented. "Men and women bore their own offspring on their shoulders to the church and cast them into a common pit. From these came such a stench that hardly anyone cared to cross the cemeteries."

BOCCACCIO ON THE PLAGUE PSYCHE

In his lengthy introduction to *The Decameron*, Giovanni Boccaccio describes three basic approaches to the Great Mortality that he observed among his fellow citizens of Florence.

According to Boccaccio, one group of Florentines responded to the terrifying pestilence by trying to isolate themselves from the rest of society and strictly avoiding all excesses in food and drink. A second group took the opposite tack, devoting themselves to the pursuit of pleasure and embracing the hedonistic philosophy "eat, drink, and be merry, for tomorrow you die." Finally, a third group attempted to steer a middle course between the extreme behaviors adopted by the other two:

> Some people were of the opinion that a sober and abstemious [self-restrained] mode of living considerably reduced the risk of infection. They therefore formed themselves into groups and lived in isolation from everyone else. Having withdrawn to a comfortable abode where there were no sick persons, they locked themselves in and settled down to a peaceable existence, consuming modest quantities of delicate foods and precious wines and avoiding all excesses. . . .
>
> Others took the opposite view, and maintained that an infallible way of warding off this appalling evil was to drink heavily, enjoy life to the full, go round singing and merrymaking, gratify all of one's cravings whenever the opportunity offered, and shrug the whole thing off as one enormous joke. . . . But for all their riotous manner of living, these people always took good care to avoid any contact with the sick . . .
>
> There were many other people who steered a middle course between the two already mentioned, neither restricting their diet to the same degree as the first group, nor indulging so freely as the second in drinking and other forms of wantonness, but simply doing no more than satisfy their appetite. Instead of incarcerating themselves, these people moved about freely, holding in their hands a posy of flowers, or fragrant herbs, or one of a wide range of spices,

Italian poet Giovanni Boccaccio *(above)* lost family and close friends to the plague, which inspired him to write his most famous work, *The Decameron*. The collection of 100 stories includes Boccaccio's observations of human behavior as people infected by the plague came to terms with their impending deaths.

which they applied at frequent intervals to their nostrils, thinking it an excellent idea to fortify the brain with smells of that particular sort; for the stench of dead bodies . . . seemed to fill and pollute the whole of the atmosphere.

A JUST PUNISHMENT FROM GOD

In his analysis of the plague psyche in Florence, Boccaccio paid little attention to the issue of religion. Yet many Catholic Europeans, clergymen and laypersons alike, saw a close connection between the plague and their Christian beliefs. The deadly pandemic, they were convinced, was a direct punishment from God for what they considered as the moral shortcomings of their generation. As Joseph Byrne points out in his book *The Black Death*, "The idea that God would use pestilence to punish the wicked . . . is firmly rooted in the Bible." In the Hebrew scriptures (the Old Testament to Christians), God frequently punishes or threatens to punish sinners with dreadful illnesses, including leprosy, a particularly gruesome disease that attacks the skin, nervous system, and eyes.

Medieval commentators tied the Almighty's wrath with the people of Europe to a wide range of sinful behavior, including greed, vanity, lust, drunkenness, pride, dishonesty, and blasphemy (speaking disrespectfully of God or the church). Henry Knighton, an English monk and chronicler of the plague, maintained that God had sent the Great Mortality because many of Europe's female inhabitants had been dressing immodestly in recent years. In his native country, Knighton observed disapprovingly, "Whenever and wherever tournaments [mock battles between knights] were held, a troupe of ladies would turn up dressed in a variety of male clothing . . . and mounted on chargers. There were sometimes as many as forty or fifty of them, representing the showiest and most beautiful, though not most virtuous, women of the realm. . . [They] wore thick belts studded with gold and silver slung across their hips, below the navel . . . and were deaf to the demands of modesty." In response to this depraved behavior, Knighton coldly declared, "God, present in these things, as in everything, supplied *a marvelous remedy*," in other words, the Black Death.

Some churchmen even suggested that children, who died in great numbers during the Black Death, might have been specifically targeted for their sinful behavior by the plague's divine author. One Catholic cleric thought he had the answer

Interpreting the Black Death as Divine Punishment

In his *Historia de Morbo*, the fourteenth-century Italian writer Gabriel de Mussis included a passage in which God expresses his frustration with mankind's apparently "limitless capacity for evil" right before sending the plague to Earth:

> Almighty God, . . . looked down from heaven and saw the entire human race wallowing in the mire of manifold wickedness, enmeshed in wrongdoing, pursuing numberless vices, drowning in a sea of depravity because of a limitless capacity for evil, bereft of all goodness, not fearing the judgements [sic] of God, and chasing after everything evil, regardless of how hateful and loathsome it was. Seeing such things He called out to the earth: "What are you doing, held captive by gangs of worthless men, soiled with the filth of sinners?"

to the dilemma of why Europe's youngest inhabitants should have been hit so hard by the Great Mortality. "It may be that it is in vengeance of this sin of dishonoring and despising of fathers and mothers that God is slaying children by pestilence, as you see daily," the seemingly hard-hearted priest wrote.

Looking back to the months and weeks before the Black Death erupted, many European Christians recalled a number of heavenly portents, or signs, that should have forewarned them that God was preparing to send something bad their way. The Belgian astronomer Simon de Covinus realized that he

Like many Catholic Europeans of his time, de Mussis clearly viewed the Black Death as divine punishment for human sinfulness. Yet many medieval Muslims were also convinced that the plague was God's punishment for human immorality. While some Muslim commentators in the Middle East and southern Spain (which had a substantial Muslim population during the fourteenth century) emphasized the importance of medicine in combating the plague, many others stressed the vital role of sincere repentance and prayer in overcoming the terrible scourge. When the city of Damascus in modern-day Syria was struck by the Black Death, great public religious rituals and prayer meetings went on for days. "We ask God's forgiveness for our soul's bad inclination," wrote the Muslim chronicler of the plague, Ibn al-Wardi. "The plague is surely part of His punishment. . . . We seek Your protection, Oh Lord of creation, from the blows of this stick. We ask for Your mercy which is wider than our sins even as they are the number of the sands and pebbles. . . . Protect us from the evil and the torture and preserve us. . . ."

had observed an unusual number of shooting stars in the night sky directly before the outbreak. In Paris, some people remembered having seen what appeared to be a ball of fire above the city. In Venice, a small earthquake that caused the bells of the famed St. Mark's Cathedral to clang eerily reputedly heralded the coming of the Great Mortality. In Yorkshire, England, according to one local chronicler, the arrival of the pestilence was foreshadowed by the birth of "a human monster" who was "divided from the naval upwards and both masculine and feminine, and joined in the lower part."

WHIPPING THE PLAGUE AWAY: THE FLAGELLANT MOVEMENT

To the modern mind, one of the strangest psychological responses to the Black Death was the flagellant movement of 1348–1350. The flagellants, whose name comes from the Latin word for whip—*flagellum*—were fervent believers in the theory that the Great Mortality was God's punishment for human sinfulness. To show the Almighty that they were repentant and to appease His righteous wrath, the flagellants publicly and savagely whipped themselves and each other with knotted cords at least three times a day. According to one eyewitness, the flagellants further cut and bruised their bodies by assembling large piles of stones and sharp nettles onto which they "dropped like logs, flat on their belly and face, with arms outstretched"—mimicking Jesus on the cross. Members of the movement were supposed to travel from town to town, flogging themselves, singing hymns, and praying, for at least 33-and-a-half days, corresponding to the number of years that Jesus is traditionally said to have spent on Earth. During this period, the flagellants were not allowed to change their torn, blood-stained clothing or wash their lacerated skin.

Most scholars believe that the gory flagellant processions of the Black Death era began in Austria sometime during the autumn of 1348. Soon the grisly pageants had spread into

Hungary, Poland, Germany, France, Flanders, and Holland. By July of 1349, the movement had attracted as many as a million followers in central and western Europe, according to some estimates.

By this point, the head of the Catholic Church, Pope Clement VI, had become gravely concerned about the flagellants. As the flagellants wandered from town to town, their leaders often preached to the large crowds who gathered to gawk at their bizarre performances. This deeply disturbed the pope

A Description of the Flagellants

The flagellant movement did not begin during the Black Death; flagellant processions had taken place in famine-stricken Italy and central Europe during the early 1260s. Yet the horrors of the Great Mortality brought the bizarre practice unprecedented popularity. In 1349, the German chronicler Henry of Herford wrote a graphic description of the flagellant group that passed through his hometown and the cruel, metal-tipped whips they used to scourge themselves:

> Each whip consisted of a stick with three knotted thongs hanging from the end. Two pieces of needle-sharp metal were run through the center of the knots from both sides, forming a cross. . . . Using these whips they beat and whipped their bare skin until their bodies were bruised and swollen and blood rained down, spattering the walls nearby. I have seen, when they whipped themselves, how sometimes those bits of metal penetrated the flesh so deeply that it took more than two attempts to pull them out.

and the rest of the Catholic hierarchy because preaching was supposed to be restricted to members of the clergy, and the flagellant movement was made up primarily of laypersons. Moreover, some flagellants were openly critical of the Catholic Church and its clergy; in one notorious incident in Flanders, a mob (after allegedly being egged on by the flagellants) murdered a local priest for daring to bar the movement from his parish. Consequently, in October 1349, Pope Clement officially condemned the flagellants for flouting church teachings and authority and ordered local bishops and political leaders to stop the processions at once, by whatever means necessary. Rulers across the continent, including King Philip VI of France and King Manfred of Sicily, hastily complied with the pope's edict, threatening flagellants with arrest or even execution. By the end of 1350, the once wildly popular movement had all but disappeared from Europe. The flagellants, observed one medieval chronicler, "vanished as suddenly as they had come, like night phantoms or mocking ghosts."

ANTI-SEMITISM AND THE PLAGUE PSYCHE: BLAMING THE JEWS

Not all Christian Europeans blamed their own—or their neighbors' sinfulness—for the plague, however. Instead, they blamed the Jews. The largest cultural minority in Europe, Jews had long been the scapegoats for medieval Christians when anything really horrible happened. So it is hardly surprising that as the plague was sweeping through Europe in the late 1340s, rumors were rife that a Jewish conspiracy was behind the mysterious and deadly pestilence. The most widely circulated story was that Jews, bent on world domination, were poisoning the wells of Christian cities and towns all over the continent. Allegedly, the Jews had used black magic to concoct the plague-causing poison from such ingredients as frogs, lizards, spiders, the hearts of murdered Christians, and the skin of a basilisk, a mythical and highly deadly snake.

Believing the plague to be God's punishment for the sins of mankind, groups of people began traveling across Europe, whipping themselves three times a day with knotted ropes. Known as the flagellants, these zealots abused themselves as an act of repentance.

From 1348—soon after the Black Death arrived in western Europe—until 1351—the year that the pandemic withdrew from most of the continent—Jews were slaughtered in dozens of European communities. The first pogroms (organized massacres of Jews) occurred in southern France, where men, women, and children were pulled out of their homes by angry mobs and burned alive. From there, the anti-Semitic violence spread northward and eastward. In Basle, Switzerland, in January 1349, the city's entire Jewish population were taken to a nearby island, locked in a specially constructed wooden building, and incinerated. The people of Speyer in southwestern Germany, worried that even dead Jews were capable of spreading the plague, encased the bodies of those they killed into empty wine barrels and rolled them into the Rhine River. Just to the north in Mainz, home to the biggest Jewish community in Europe, 6,000 Jews reportedly died on a single day in August 1349. In a number of German towns, Jews, convinced that it was only a matter of time before Christian mobs came for them, decided to take their own lives. For example, in December 1349, Esslingen's Jewish residents committed mass suicide by shutting themselves into their synagogue and setting it ablaze.

Pope Clement was appalled by the murderous pogroms against the Jews—and the looting and confiscation of Jewish property that inevitably accompanied them. In 1348, he issued two formal proclamations prohibiting the vicious and unlawful attacks. In his second proclamation, Clement declared that Catholics who believed that the Jews were responsible for the Great Mortality had been "seduced by that liar, the Devil." It made no sense to blame Jews for the pestilence, the pope pointed out, since they, too, were dying in droves from the mysterious illness.

In France and Italy, anti-Semitic violence all but disappeared following the pontiff's proclamations. However, Clement's call for an end to the pogroms seems to have been largely ignored in Germany and Switzerland, where the attacks continued until the pandemic began to fade away around 1350. In the meantime, when Duke Casimir II of Poland, a loyal defender of his own kingdom's Jewish population, offered persecuted Jews from other parts of Europe sanctuary in his sparsely populated domain, large numbers of Jews, particularly from Germany, gratefully accepted his offer. In time, many of these Black Death refugees would filter back westward. Yet, in Germany as elsewhere in central and western Europe, notes historian

Barbara Tuchman, the Jews "returned to live in weakened and fearful communities on worse terms and in greater segregation than ever before. . . . The walls of the ghetto [enclosed quarters in European cities to which Jews were eventually restricted], though not yet physical, had risen."

5 Medieval Medicine and the Black Death

When the Great Mortality arrived in Europe in the late 1340s, the medical community did not know what to make of the mysterious and highly lethal pandemic. Many physicians accepted the popular view that the plague was God's punishment for human wickedness and people could do little to combat it except to repent of their sins. Influenced by the theories of two respected ancient authorities, the fourth-century B.C. Greek physician Hippocrates and the second-century Greco-Roman physician Galen, other doctors attributed the Black Death to natural causes, however.

POISONOUS VAPORS AND PLANETARY MOVEMENTS

According to the teachings of Galen and Hippocrates, disease arose from thick clouds of poisoned air called miasmas, which people either breathed in or absorbed through their skin. These noxious vapors were supposedly released into the atmosphere by fetid swamps, dung heaps, cesspools, decaying animal carcasses, and unburied human corpses. In addition to the sources of miasma identified by Galen and Hippocrates in their writings, some fourteenth-century physicians believed that certain changes in the positions of the heavenly bodies could also taint the Earth's atmosphere with disease-causing mists.

Like the ancient Greeks and Romans, whose learning and civilizations they admired, medieval physicians and scholars were convinced there was a close relationship between earthly happenings and the planets and stars they observed in the night sky. They considered astrology (the study of the shifting positions of the celestial bodies to determine their supposed effect on natural and human events) as a genuine branch of science. Given medieval Europeans' high regard for astrology, it is hardly surprising that when King Philip VI of France ordered the continent's foremost medical authorities—the faculty of the Paris College of Physicians—to research the pestilence's origins, their findings focused primarily on planetary movements.

In their published treatise (essay) on the Great Mortality, *Compendium de Epidemia* (Account of the Epidemic), the Paris dons placed the pandemic's beginnings at 1:00 in the afternoon on March 20, 1345. At that exact moment, the orbits of three planets—Mars, Jupiter, and Saturn—lined up in the 40th degree of Aquarius, one of the 12 astrological constellations of the zodiac (an imaginary heavenly belt). According to the scholars, this rare coming together of the three planets created a human health disaster of cataclysmic proportions. The conjunction of Saturn and Jupiter portended widespread suffering and death on Earth, they explained. At the same time, they wrote, the conjunction of humid Jupiter and fiery Mars released vile, disease-producing vapors into the atmosphere. Adding to the huge quantities of corrupted air created by the alignment of Mars and Jupiter was miasma from earthly sources such as swamps, cesspools, or rotting cadavers.

STAYING WELL

If the pestilence was caused by miasma, as the professors asserted, then it followed that the best protection against the illness was to avoid the poisoned air as much as possible. In their treatise on the Great Mortality, the faculty of the Paris College of Physicians included a number of suggestions for steering clear of plague-inducing vapors. Miasma, they declared, was generally carried by warm, humid winds blowing in from the south. Therefore, people should keep the windows on the south sides of their houses tightly closed and locked. For added security, the windows "should be protected with a border of coated string [caulking], so that air cannot enter the apartment, unless the . . . air blows in the middle of the day, when it is purified by the heat of the sun," proclaimed the authors of *Compendium de Epidemia*. On the other hand, because the cool north wind cleansed the air of impurities, the learned doctors declared, north-facing windows should be kept open whenever practicable.

Another excellent preventive against disease-causing vapors was inhaling aromatics, according to the *Compendium*. People were urged to scatter pleasantly scented herbs, spices, and flower petals around their houses. When they ventured beyond their houses, they could fill their pockets with the fragrant and supposedly protective substances. Alternatively, people could hold "smelling apples" underneath their noses as a preventive against breathing in poisoned air. Also called amber apples they were made from aromatics such as amber, musk, rosemary, and black pepper that had been soaked in rosewater for a week and molded into round bundles using gum arabic (a sticky substance obtained from the acacia tree). Building bonfires from pungent woods like juniper or pine to drive away noxious fumes from larger areas was also recommended. In direct opposition to the advice of the Paris medical scholars, some medieval physicians thought that foul rather than pleasant odors were the best way to keep the Great Mortality at bay.

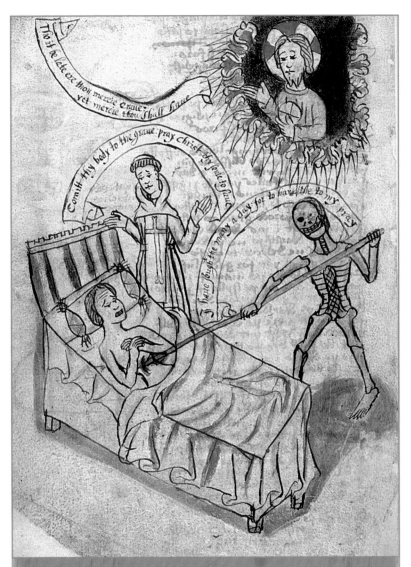

Before the bacterium that caused bubonic plague was identified, many theories existed regarding the source of infection. To avoid the plague, some people prayed harder; others tried to ward off the deadly spirit they believed was to blame; and doctors advised people to seal their windows in order to avoid vapors. In the illustration above, a priest delivers last rites to a plague victim.

Consequently, it was not unusual during the Black Death to see large groups of people in stricken towns leaning over the edge of the community latrine and inhaling deeply!

In their treatise on the plague, the faculty of the Paris College of Physicians also emphasized careful monitoring of personal bathing, exercise, and eating habits. Hot baths, they warned, should be avoided at all costs. Soaking in warm water opened the skin's pores, making it easier for infected vapors to enter the body, the scholars explained. People should also refrain from running or other forms of intense exercise because the rapid, heavy breathing caused by hard physical exertion increased their chances of inhaling contaminated air. "On the subject of eating and drinking," the authors of *Compendium de Epidemia* declared:

> We have observed that one should avoid all excesses of food and drink because humid things are predisposed to the epidemic. One should eat lightly, choosing food that is easily digested and capable of enriching the blood such as bread made with a high-quality tender wheat . . . and mixed with a little bran and barley. Among meats, it is necessary to choose lambs of one year, tender pieces of veal, kid [young goat], rabbits, young chickens, hens, partridges, pheasant, starlings, capons, and small birds. . . .

OTHER CONTAGION THEORIES: EVIL EYES AND ACCIDENTS OF THE SOUL

Although the dons of the Paris College of Physicians maintained that people caught the plague by breathing infected vapors into their lungs, other medieval doctors believed that the contagion could also be spread directly from person to person. Some of their theories on how the plague traveled from one individual to another were highly imaginative. For example, some physicians declared that the infected could spread the disease to others just by looking at them, in effect, by giving them the evil eye. Others asserted that people could contract the disease merely by touching a plague victim or any of his or her belongings. In Montpellier, France, one doctor was convinced that a malicious, plague-bearing "air spirit" passed from his stricken patients to their healthy family members and visitors, usually right before the patients died.

Perhaps the most bizarre theory regarding how people became infected with the plague centered on what medieval medical tracts referred to as "accidents of the soul," by which they meant negative emotions such as fear, anxiety, and grief. According to this hypothesis, individuals could literally think themselves into sickness. Spanish physician Jacme d'Agramont, one leading supporter of the "mind over matter" theory, explained: "From imagination alone can come any malady. . . . Thus, it is evidently very dangerous and perilous in times of pestilence to imagine death and to have fear." Perhaps, speculated historian John Aberth in *From the Brink of the Apocalypse: Confronting Famine, War, Plague, and Death in the Later Middle Ages*, the belief that morbid thoughts made people susceptible to the Great Mortality was behind the unusual ordinances passed by the plague-stricken Italian cities of Florence, Venice, and Pistoia. When the municipal councils of the three cities prohibited the ringing of church bells or the wearing of black clothing at funerals in the summer of 1348, Aberth suggested, they may have been motivated by a desire to calm their citizens' "unhealthy" fears by downplaying the communities' mounting death tolls.

"TO FLEE . . . IS BEST"

Most medieval physicians agreed that the surest way to avoid getting the plague—whether it was spread by noxious fumes in the atmosphere or directly from person to person—was flight. Gentile da Foligno, a professor of medicine at the University of Padua in northeast Italy, advised people living in plague-stricken areas to leave at once, go far, and stay away a long

Though doctors in the Middle Ages usually dressed themselves in expensive clothing denoting their profession and class, some began to wear special costumes during the sixteenth-century plague epidemic. This outfit included a waxed robe, protective gloves and boots, a leather hat, and a mask featuring a large beak filled with spices and flowers to ward off disease-causing "vapors."

time. "To flee . . . is best in this particular pestilence; for this illness is the most poisonous of poisons, and by its spread and blight it affects all," da Foligno wrote in 1348, while the Great Mortality was consuming his native town of Perugia.

A number of Europeans, most of them wealthy city-dwellers, did follow da Foligno's advice, abandoning their homes for remote and sparsely populated areas in the countryside. Yet because the plague ravaged rural as well as urban areas, the Great Mortality eventually caught up with many of them anyway. Gentile da Foligno failed to follow his own advice, heroically staying at his post despite the risks. He died in Perugia in June 1348, though the cause, whether from the pestilence or from exhaustion, is a matter of debate among historians. Da Foligno was not alone in his deep commitment to his patients. During the Black Death, the mortality rate among physicians, especially on the Italian Peninsula and in France, was staggering. For instance, the Italian city of Piacenza reportedly lost 20 of its 24 doctors to the plague, while in Montpellier, France, according to one eyewitness, "There was a greater number of physicians than elsewhere, yet scarce one escaped alive."

CURES: BLOODLETTING AND SNAKE MEAT

During the Great Mortality, most published medical tracts advised treating plague patients in one of two different ways: by bloodletting to purge plague-causing poisons from the body or with exotic elixirs to neutralize the poisons within the body. Virtually all the medical pamphlets placed enormous importance on prayer, both for physical healing and forgiveness for past sins. Jacme d'Agramont wrote that before beginning any treatment regimens, doctors should encourage their patients to acknowledge their "sins and . . . failings by hearty repentance and oral confession . . ."

Following in the tradition of the Greek physicians Hippocrates and Galen, and the celebrated eleventh-century Persian scholar Avicenna, medieval medicine taught that the

Physicians' Attire During the Black Death

Many people associate the Black Death pandemic of the mid-fourteenth century with illustrations of medieval physicians outfitted in strange, beaked masks as they tended to their plague-stricken patients. In fact, the frightening-looking doctors' masks did not appear in Europe until the sixteenth century during a subsequent plague epidemic. The masks' long, leather "beaks" were typically packed with sweet-smelling herbs and spices that were thought to protect against harmful exhalations from ill patients. Along with the raven-like masks, some sixteenth-century physicians also donned wide-brimmed hats, gloves, and long robes fashioned from a special waxed fabric before visiting plague victims. The rationale behind the waxed robes was that disease-causing particles in the air would not stick to the slippery material, thus helping to guard the doctor from infection.

There is no evidence that European physicians relied on specially designed, protective masks or clothing when tending to plague patients during the Black Death pandemic of the late 1340s and early 1350s. According to a contemporary Italian account, fourteenth-century physicians typically dressed to impress, adorning themselves in long, richly colored robes with fur-trimmed hoods; elegant, embroidered gloves; and belts finished with silver thread. Many physicians, however, probably carried fragrant petals and leaves or "smelling apples" with them on their house visits as a preventive against breathing in poisoned fumes.

human body contained four humors, or fluids: blood, yellow bile, black bile, and phlegm. Each of these bodily fluids corresponded to one of the four basic elements: blood was equated with air, yellow bile with fire, black bile with earth, and phlegm with water. In a healthy individual, the four humors were in balance. When plague invaded the body, medieval physicians believed, the humors—and particularly the blood—were corrupted by the poison and became unstable. The standard treatment for this condition was bloodletting: opening the veins with a sharp knife to draw the tainted blood away from vital organs such as the heart, brain, and liver and to restore the balance of the humors. The bloodletting should continue, advised Gentile da Foligno, until the patient became light-headed or actually lost consciousness altogether.

Antidotes that supposedly neutralized the plague "poison" surging through a victim's bloodstream were also popular during the Black Death. Medieval doctors often prescribed elixirs containing finely ground precious metals and gems, although only their wealthiest patients could afford to purchase such expensive medicines. According to one medical tract, molten (liquefied) gold was the best antidote against the pestilence because it was capable of purifying any poison, no matter how strong. Gentile da Foligno, on the other hand, thought that nothing worked better against the plague than finely ground emerald powder, a remedy so powerful he once asserted, that it could "crack a toad's eyes."

The most widely prized—and hard to come by—of the various plague antidotes, because of its exotic and rare ingredients, was theriac. Although there were many different recipes for theriac, all of them featured snake meat, usually roasted and mashed or finely chopped. Other theriac ingredients might include anything from the heart and hooves of a stag to silver, coral, or Armenian clay. The king of Portugal's personal physician had a theriac recipe called "badger

Some plague physicians practiced bloodletting on their patients *(depicted above)*, cutting into their veins in order to release supposedly tainted blood from the body. Similar procedures involved the use of leeches, which were placed on a patient in an attempt to remove the infected blood and reestablish the balance of humors or fluids in the body.

powder." It featured the blood and liver of the burrowing, nocturnal animal. In order to ensure the most potent concoction possible, the Portuguese physician suggested, before the badger was slaughtered it should be forced to drink large amounts of wine mixed with seed pearls and ground gold.

PUBLIC HEALTH MEASURES TO COMBAT THE BLACK DEATH

During the Black Death, some towns and city-states, particularly in northern and central Italy, attempted to stop the outbreak in its tracks through a host of public health measures. Sadly, these measures would prove largely ineffective against the deadly and rapidly spreading pandemic.

Among the first of the Italian city-states to adopt stringent public health regulations in the face of the Black Death was wealthy and cultured Florence. As the plague approached Florence from the west early in the spring of 1348, city authorities began frantically passing ordinances designed to keep the pestilence at bay. Florentines were directed to keep their homes, shops, streets, and yards as clean as possible, and a 500-lire fine—a large sum of money—was imposed on visitors from the plague-stricken cities of Genoa and Pisa. Clearly convinced that the pestilence was spread by poisoned vapors as well as from person to person, the government also authorized special teams of inspectors to scour Florence's neighborhoods and forcibly "remove all putrid [rotten] matter and infected persons from which might arise . . . a corruption or infection of the air."

Despite these stern measures, in early April 1348 the plague struck Florence with a vengeance. By September, when it had finally run its course in the city, the Black Death had claimed some 60,000 souls, or a little more than half of the population. Boccaccio vividly described Florence's appalling death toll in *The Decameron*: "Such was the multitude of corpses that huge trenches were excavated in the churchyards, into which new arrivals were placed in their hundreds, stored tier upon tier like ships' cargo, each layer of corpses being covered with a thin layer of soil till the trench was filled to the top."

In other plague-stricken Italian cities, including Venice and Pistoia, municipal authorities issued public health measures with equally disappointing results. Venetian officials quarantined all newly arrived ships for 40 days, setting ablaze all vessels suspected of harboring the dreaded pestilence. Laws were also passed stipulating that plague victims must be buried far from the heart of the city on uninhabited islands;

Unsanitary Living Conditions in 14th-Century Europe

In her classic study of late medieval Europe, *A Distant Mirror: The Calamitous 14th Century*, historian Barbara Tuchman described the unsanitary living conditions that prevailed in most of Europe when the Black Death struck the continent in the late 1340s:

> Sewage disposal was . . . far from adequate. Privies, cesspools, drainage pipes, and public latrines existed, though they did not replace open street sewers. Castles and wealthy town houses had privies built into bays jutting from an outside wall with a hole in the bottom allowing the deposit to fall into a river or into a ditch for subsequent removal. Town houses away from the riverbank had cesspools in the backyard at a regulated distance from the neighbor's. Although supposedly constructed under town ordinances, they frequently seeped into well and other water sources. . . .
>
> During the plague, as street cleaners and carters [haulers of garbage] died, cities grew befouled, increasing the infection. Residents of a street might rent a cart in common to remove the waste, but energy and will were depressed. The breakdown in street-cleaning appears in a letter of [King] Edward III to the Mayor of London in 1349, complaining that the streets and lanes of London were "foul with human feces and the air of the city poisoned to the great danger of men passing, especially in this time of infectious disease."

the corpses were conveyed by special municipal barges. Despite the government's efforts to keep the Great Mortality at bay, however, Venice's death toll from the plague has been estimated at 72,000, or about 60 percent of the total population. In Pistoia, so that no poisonous fumes could escape from the cadavers into the air, the municipal government ordered that the remains of plague victims "shall not be removed from the place of death until they have been enclosed in a wooden box and the lid of the planks nailed down." Nonetheless, as the year 1348 drew to a close, a chronicler of the plague in Pistoia noted mournfully that "hardly a person was left alive."

6

Social and Economic Impact of the Black Death

Between 1346 and 1352, the Black Death swept away at least one-third and possibly as much as 60 percent of the continent's total population. Inevitably, the mass depopulation caused by the pandemic and subsequent plague epidemics of the late fourteenth and early fifteenth centuries had a significant impact on Europe's economy and society.

SHORT-TERM ECONOMIC EFFECTS OF THE BLACK DEATH

The chief short-term effect of the Black Death, most scholars agree, was shock. The emotional trauma caused by the staggering death toll shattered normal work routines, severely disrupting the pattern of European economic life. High mortality rates and the desertion of plague-infested cities and towns by terrified inhabitants meant that many critical tasks went unperformed. All over Europe, shops were boarded up and farm fields and livestock left unattended. Demoralized by the death and suffering all around them, even healthy workers failed to carry out their usual duties when the plague struck. According to Boccaccio's *The Decameron*, when the Great Mortality invaded the city-state of Florence during the

78

spring of 1348, peasants and townspeople alike "became lax in their ways and neglected their chores as if they expected death that very day."

Another short-term effect of the Black Death was the unprecedented demand it created for certain types of services. Plague-ravished cities and towns faced urgent shortages of physicians and apothecaries (druggists) to treat the ill, lawyers and notaries to draw up and certify wills, clergymen to provide last rites to the dying and spiritual comfort to the bereaved, and gravediggers to bury the mountains of corpses.

With dozens—sometimes hundreds—of people perishing each day in some places, the need for gravediggers was especially urgent. Fearful of being exposed to the poisoned fumes that were widely believed to seep out of infected cadavers, few people were willing to take on the job of disposing of the dead. Consequently, those on the bottommost rungs of medieval society were recruited for the unpopular task, including the rural poor, beggars, and common criminals. According to Boccaccio, the coffins of the Black Death's Florentine victims were not borne to the graveyard by their families or friends, as had long been the custom. Instead the dead were unceremoniously carted off by the *becchini*: a "kind of grave digging fraternity . . . drawn from the lowest orders of society, " Boccaccio complained in his introduction to *The Decameron*. The becchini, he wrote, "assumed the title of sexton [an official who cared for church property] and demanded a fat fee for their services, which consisted of taking up the coffin and hauling it away swiftly not to the church specified by the dead man in his will, but usually to the nearest at hand." Florence's opportunistic new brotherhood of gravediggers preyed on the city's vulnerable inhabitants like vultures, noted John Kelly in *The Great Mortality*, quickly earning

an unsavory reputation not only for their cavalier [disdainful] attitude toward death, the way they seemed almost to condescend to it, but also for their swashbuckling behavior. In a city swollen with grief and loss, the becchini drank and wenched and caroused and stole like happy buccaneers. As spring became summer, the terrors of life in Florence grew to include a front door bursting open in the dead of night and a group of drunken, shovel-wielding gravediggers rushing into the house, threatening rape and murder unless the inhabitants paid a ransom.

Gravediggers were not the only ones who callously sought to profit from the pandemic. "Servants, or those who took care of the ill, charged from one to three florins a day," observed Marchione di Coppo Stefani in his chronicle *Concerning a Mortality in the City of Florence in Which Many People Died.* Moreover, Stefani wrote

Because of the commonly held belief that disease-causing vapors seeped out of the corpses of plague victims, few people were willing to take on the job of digging graves during the Black Death. As a result the unpopular task typically fell to the men on the lowest rungs of society such as beggars and criminals.

The things that the sick ate, sweetmeats and sugar, seemed priceless. Sugar cost from three to eight florins a pound, . . . capons and other poultry were very expensive, and eggs cost between twelve and twenty-four pence each. . . . The mortality enriched apothecaries, doctors, poultry vendors, . . . and greengrocers, who sold poultices of mallow, nettles, mercury, and other herbs necessary to draw off the mortality.

A RISING STANDARD OF LIVING

Despite the work disruptions and high costs of certain services and goods, the economic effects of the Black Death were not entirely negative. Once Europe began to recover from the initial shock of the devastating pandemic, standards of living actually improved for a large portion of its inhabitants. During the century leading up to the Black Death, most historians concur, Europe had too many people in relation to the available resources, and poverty and malnutrition were widespread, particularly among the peasant masses. The coming of the Great Mortality in the 1340s, however, brought a new prosperity to many of the lower- and middle-class Europeans fortunate enough to survive the pandemic.

As Europe's population plummeted during the Black Death pandemic, severe labor shortages developed, especially in the countryside. The increasingly scarce farmworkers demanded—and grudgingly received—higher wages and lower rent payments from the landed nobility who had long held sway over Europe's economy and society. On the Italian Peninsula, the labor shortage became so pressing that many great landowners began providing workers with free housing, tools, seed, and farmland in exchange for labor on the fields. In addition, tenants were given a fixed percentage of the profits their landlord earned from the crops the laborers planted and harvested for him. According to contemporary plague chronicler Matteo Villani, peasants in the central Italian region of Tuscany stubbornly refused to work for a landlord unless he provided not only seed and tools but also oxen. Oxen significantly increased the field-workers' productivity—and profits—by enabling them to plow more acreage in a shorter period of time.

In some parts of England, laborers' wages increased four- or fivefold over a period of just a few years. For example, at Cuxham Manor in Oxfordshire, farmworkers' wages rose from about 2 shillings a week in 1347 to more than 10 shillings a week in 1350. Archaeologists excavating the English countryside have found evidence for the rising standard of living enjoyed by the kingdom's rural masses following the Great Mortality in the types of cookware owned by peasants before and after the plague struck. Before the Black Death, the vast majority of rural families relied on humble earthenware pots to cook their meals. During the decades following the pandemic, however, an increasing number of households used more costly metal cookware, the archaeologists discovered.

RESPONSES TO THE PEASANT LABOR SHORTAGE FROM ABOVE

Dismayed by the swelling cost of labor in the kingdom, England's royal government tried to regulate the wages employers could offer their workers. In June 1349, about a year after the plague reached the British Isles, King Edward III issued the Ordinance of Laborers, freezing workers' wages at pre-plague levels. Enforcement of the law was left to employers, who quickly discovered that the new legislation was impracticable. Increasingly mobile and self-assured, most workers refused to remain with an employer who paid less than the going rate. The workers were confident that if their old employer failed to meet their demands, they could easily find a new one who would. "Laborers were so elated and contentious that they did not pay attention to the command of the King," observed English monk Henry Knighton, regarding Edward III's edict.

In 1351, Parliament, England's upper-class-controlled legislative body, passed a second and harsher law aimed at bringing workers' inflated wages back to pre–Black Death levels. Enforcement of the new Statute of Laborers was placed in the hands of government officials, and secret work agreements between employers and workers were explicitly forbidden. Workers, the statute proclaimed, had to accept any wages and terms offered by an employer or face stiff fines and even imprisonment. Yet ongoing labor shortages throughout the 1350s and 1360s made it virtually impossible to enforce the tough new legislation in most parts of the kingdom. As was true in 1349, many employers quietly ignored the government-imposed wage controls for fear of losing their entire workforce. Nor was the royal government of England's plague-devastated neighbor, France, successful in imposing wage ceilings on its laborers. A French statute of 1349 freezing wages to pre–Black Death levels was largely disregarded by employers and landlords who were desperate for workers and tenants. Because of continuing labor shortfalls, similar laws passed in various parts of Germany and the Italian Peninsula during the second half of the fourteenth century also proved difficult to enforce.

Despite the failure of government-sponsored wage controls, a few great landowners, particularly in England, managed to keep their labor costs in check after the Black Death pandemic by changing how they used their chief resource: land. As the costs of maintaining a big workforce skyrocketed, these farsighted landowners abandoned agriculture for animal husbandry, especially sheep raising. Raising sheep for their meat and fleece, the landlords reasoned, required significantly fewer workers than growing wheat and other agricultural crops, since one or two sheepherders and a few dogs could easily supervise hundreds of the docile animals. Converting farm fields, particularly less fertile ones, into pastureland allowed individual landowners to remain financially solvent. It also helped to create a more diversified economy in England by boosting the island's infant wool industry. Over a span of just a dozen years, England's yearly exports of wool cloth grew more than tenfold, from about 1,000 bolts in 1350 to nearly 11,000 bolts by 1362.

THE BLACK DEATH AND SERFDOM

For centuries before the Black Death outbreak, most European peasants had been serfs, meaning that they and their descendants were legally bound to their lord's estate and owed him labor obligations along with various dues. In return, serfs received protection and the right to use a plot of their lord's land to grow their own food. By the late 1340s, when the Great Mortality first appeared on the continent, serfdom was already on the decline in much of western Europe. Many of the traditional dues that peasants owed to their master, such as marriage or birth taxes, were gradually being reduced or even cut altogether. Many scholars, however, believe that the plague pandemic greatly accelerated the decay of serfdom. According to Robert Gottfried, the depopulation caused by the Black Death and subsequent plague epidemics of the late fourteenth and early fifteenth centuries "virtually ended serfdom in western Europe." As Gottfried wrote in his book *The Black Death: Natural and Human Disaster in Medieval Europe*:

> For the first time in centuries, peasants were mobile enough to pick up and move from one manor to the next if they were unhappy with the conditions under which they held their land. A peasant could leave in the middle of the night, go to the next manor, and expect to be welcomed, so short was the supply of labor. Any lord who hoped to keep his workers had to offer them better terms of tenure than they had had before the Black Death. By the 1360s, this had resulted in much lower rents in most of western Europe. This development was followed by the commutation of traditional labor . . . services, that is, the substitution of cash

payments for old labor services. Then, in the course of the fifteenth century, most of the other labor services . . . were eliminated, replaced by money rates and long-term leases. In effect, while the lords still owned the land or held it of a higher lord, they did so with hired labor rather than unfree peasants. . . . The peasant worked all the land he could and paid only rent.

Yet serfdom did not fade away in every part of Europe following the Black Death. In eastern Europe, the oppressive system of labor actually became more widespread in the wake of the Great Mortality. Probably because of the area's comparatively limited commercial ties with the outside world and smaller, more dispersed population, eastern Europe was hit less hard by the plague than other parts of the continent. Moreover, in part because of the labor shortages and economic disruptions caused by the Black Death in western Europe, by about 1350 Poland, Hungary, Prussia (today eastern Germany), and Russia had emerged as Europe's "breadbasket," supplying a large portion of the continent's grain needs. Relying on underpaid serfs to till their vast grain farms allowed eastern European landowners to maximize their profits, and the great lords did not hesitate to use brute force to keep their heavily exploited workforce in line.

A CRISIS FOR THE NOBILITY

Although the landed nobility of eastern Europe generally prospered after the Black Death, for many western European nobles the pandemic was an economic and social disaster. Noble incomes fell sharply as labor costs rose, rent payments shrank, and other traditional dues paid by peasant tenants were severely reduced or eliminated. These financial losses might have been largely offset by higher prices for the lords' agricultural crops. But following a brief surge in food prices directly after the plague struck, prices for most agricultural

Sumptuary Laws and the Black Death

One way in which Europe's noble class attempted to hold on to their position in medieval society was through pressing their governments to pass sumptuary laws. Designed to reinforce traditional divisions between the classes, sumptuary laws specified what styles of clothes could be worn by non-aristocrats in an effort to prevent newly prosperous commoners from trying to ape their social "betters."

The new laws, which were enacted all across Europe during the late fourteenth and early fifteenth centuries, sought to regulate everything from the lengths of the trains on women's gowns to what type of animal fur an individual could wear in public. With rising incomes among the lower and middle classes, as Robert Gottfried explained in his book *The Black Death: Natural and Human Disaster in Medieval Europe*, "Furs . . . were now affordable for more people than at any time in centuries." Convinced that furs were still an elite status symbol and ought to reflect the wearer's social standing, medieval authorities were dismayed by this turn of events. In response to the widespread wearing of furs among Englishmen and women of all socioeconomic classes during the decade following the Black Death, in 1363 the English parliament passed a sumptuary law proclaiming that only nobles could don the most highly valued furs such as sable. Well-off commoners were prohibited from wearing anything more luxurious than lambskin, and laborers were ordered to wear only cat or rabbit fur. Not surprisingly, England's new regulations regarding the wearing of fur, like most of the other sumptuary laws passed in Europe after the Black Death, proved virtually impossible to enforce.

crops began to fall, reflecting the fact that there were now fewer mouths to feed in Europe. In order to avoid total ruin, some nobles sought another source of income aside from farming, most often from positions in the Catholic Church or the army. Others tried to improve their financial standing through marriage to a well-off commoner. In a desperate effort to hold on to their estates, some nobles in central Italy even resorted to banditry or hired out their military services to rival city-states as soldiers of fortune.

Many noble European families simply vanished altogether as a result of the pandemic. "Ah, how great a number of splendid palaces, fine houses, and noble dwellings, once filled with retainers [attendants], with lords and with ladies, were bereft of all who had lived there, down to the tiniest child! How numerous were the famous families, the vast estates, the notable fortunes, that were seen to be left without a rightful successor!" lamented Boccaccio in *The Decameron*. "Marriage, the production of progeny [descendants], and inheritance were the core of gentry life," explained historian Norman Cantor in his book *In the Wake of the Plague: The Black Death and the World It Made*. Yet the pandemic's high death rate wreaked havoc with this venerable economic and social system by leaving many aristocratic families without a surviving heir. "Coveted estates that had taken generations to build were suddenly swallowed by another family, distantly related, and the losing family's honorable name was expunged from society and history," wrote Cantor.

POPULAR UPRISINGS IN EUROPE AFTER THE BLACK DEATH

Although the Black Death significantly reduced the economic influence of western Europe's landed nobles, the vast political power once held by the great feudal lords had begun to dwindle long before the pandemic hit. This was especially true in France and England, where strong, centralized monarchies had developed during the first half of the fourteenth century.

Despite the growing political sway of these centralized royal governments, however, law enforcement was still largely a local affair when the Black Death reached Europe, even in France and England. Just as they had done for centuries, the landed nobility oversaw the police systems and courts of law in most communities throughout the 1400s. Distracted by their growing financial woes, however, many aristocrats neglected their policing and judicial duties after the pandemic hit, and law and order began to break down throughout much of the European countryside. "People resorted increasingly to violence to settle their differences," contended Robert Gottfried, and rural crime rates skyrocketed.

The unsettled and increasingly violent atmosphere of the post-plague years contributed directly to two major popular uprisings in Europe, first in France and later in England. When the Jacquerie uprising erupted in France in the spring of 1358, the Hundred Years' War between England and France had already dragged on for more than a decade. Largely fought on French soil, the war only added to the rising tide of lawlessness that gripped the kingdom as a consequence of the Black Death. During the 1350s, following a short break in the fighting at the height of the pandemic, Spanish and other foreign mercenaries employed by the English army roamed the countryside of northern France, plundering, pillaging, and raping at will. Angered both by their landlords' inability to protect them from marauders and their landlords' refusal to compensate them for war-damaged fields and homes, peasants rose up against the aristocracy all over northern France. For nearly a month, peasant mobs vandalized and looted noble estates and slaughtered their terrorized inhabitants before government troops finally quelled the uprising. (The name given to the bloody rebellion, La Jacquerie, came from the popular use of Jacques as a generic name for all peasants in medieval France.)

A little more than 20 years after the Jacquerie uprising, Great Britain was rocked by its own peasant rebellion. The immediate cause of the Peasants' Revolt of 1381 was a new head, or poll, tax of one shilling, which the royal government, struggling to finance the ongoing Hundred Years' War, had

Two major peasant uprisings occurred in Europe during the Black Death, one in France and one in England. The revolt in France, La Jacquerie *(depicted above)*, took place during the Hundred Years' War when French nobles failed to protect the peasants from foreign mercenaries who roamed the countryside, pillaging and plundering. Angry peasant mobs looted noble estates and murdered their inhabitants for weeks before government forces finally crushed the rebellion.

levied on all English citizens over the age of 15. Most peasants deeply resented the new tax. Since it taxed everyone, rich or poor, at the same rate, the poll tax was fundamentally unjust, they contended. At the same time, the peasants worried that the increasingly cash-strapped nobility might try to reverse the economic and social gains that they had made following the pandemic, including the elimination of most of the old feudal dues and restrictions on their movements.

During the late spring of 1381, the peasants' resentments and fears exploded into violence when angry mobs in eastern England attacked local tax collectors and nobles. The uprising soon spread throughout much of the southeastern portion of the kingdom, where local lords seemed powerless to stop the growing bloodshed and looting. By June, the rebels—under the leadership of Wat Tyler, a blacksmith—had decided to march to London to present their grievances directly to England's young king, Richard II. But Tyler's peasant army proved no match for the royal forces, and when Tyler was killed, the rebellion quickly fizzled out. Determined to strike fear into the hearts of the lower class, the Crown executed thousands of peasants in reprisal for the abortive uprising. Nonetheless, the government also permanently eliminated the hated poll tax, a clear sign of the workingman's new clout in the wake of the massive population loss caused by the Black Death.

7 Religion, Culture, and the Black Death

The enormous suffering and population loss that accompanied the Black Death pandemic affected virtually every aspect of European life. Most scholars agree that the Great Mortality caused—or at least accelerated—important changes not only in the economy and social structure of Europe but also in its religion, art, and literature.

THE BLACK DEATH AND RELIGION IN MEDIEVAL EUROPE

Medieval Europeans were already a deeply religious people when the Black Death reached Italy in 1347, staunchly committed to their Christian faith and Roman Catholic Church. Nonetheless, contended John Kelly in *The Great Mortality*, in the wake of the deadly pandemic many Europeans "began to long for a more intense, personal relationship with God." One consequence of this new religious fervor was an upsurge in the building of independent chapels for private worship. Private chapels had long been popular among the landed aristocracy. But after the plague, an increasing number of well-off commoners such as merchants, physicians, and lawyers began to erect small chapels of their own. Even middle-class craftsmen took part in the chapel-building craze. Most medieval artisans belonged to guilds, associations of craftsmen organized to uphold standards in a particular trade and safeguard the interests of their memberships. By pooling their resources, a number of guilds in England and elsewhere in Europe were able to construct chapels for the exclusive use of members and their families during the late fourteenth and early fifteenth centuries.

At the same time that the Black Death was inspiring many Europeans to seek a closer, more personal relationship with God, it was exacting a terrible toll on the most powerful religious institution in all of medieval Europe: the Roman Catholic Church. As a result of the pandemic, the church lost an estimated 40 percent of its personnel, including thousands of bishops, priests, and deacons. Because their residents lived in close quarters, monasteries and convents were particularly hard hit by the Great Mortality. Some religious houses were all but obliterated during the pandemic. For example, Gherardo Petrarca, the brother of the famed Italian poet Petrarch, was the sole survivor out of the 35 monks who resided in the Carthusian monastery at Montrieux, France, when the plague struck.

Perhaps the greatest blow to the Catholic Church during the Black Death era was the large number of parish or local priests who succumbed to the plague. Parish priests played a crucial role in the functioning of the church. "Most people imbibed their faith from the parish priest they visited every Sunday," noted John Aberth in his book *From the Brink of the Apocalypse*. In addition to conducting worship services, weddings, funerals, and baptisms, the parish priest visited the sick and comforted the bereaved. The parish priest, often the only literate person in the entire community, was responsible for teaching his congregation the Holy Scriptures and church doctrine.

A letter from Bishop Ralph Shrewsbury to the priests of his diocese in Bath and Wells, England, reflected the severe personnel shortage faced by Catholic parishes across Europe in the Black Death's wake. In his letter of January 1349,

While the nobility suffered from a lack of workers, the Catholic Church was also shorthanded as whole monasteries and convents were wiped out by illness. In response, Pope Clement VI lowered the educational standards and age requirements for students training for the priesthood, hoping to bolster his small supply of clergymen.

Shrewsbury ordered the priests under his supervision to do something unheard of in the medieval church: encourage laypersons (non-clergymen) to serve as confessors for dying relatives and friends if an ordained minister was unavailable. The bishop wrote:

> The contagious pestilence, which is now spreading everywhere, has left many parish churches ... bereft of a

The Black Death and Education

The Black Death's impact on educational institutions, particularly those of higher learning, was significant. In the pandemic's wake, a number of new colleges and universities were founded throughout Europe to help train replacements for the thousands of Catholic clerics who succumbed to the plague. England's two great universities, Cambridge and Oxford, gained a total of six new colleges during the two decades following the Black Death, while major new universities were founded in Florence, Prague, Vienna, and several other cities on the European continent during the same period.

The Black Death's most significant effect on medieval education in Europe may have been within the realm of language, however. The death of scores of primary and secondary school instructors along with many university professors appears to have greatly accelerated a change in the status of national languages in Europe that had begun decades earlier. For many centuries, Latin, the tongue of the ancient Romans, had been the language of scholarship and high culture throughout most of Europe. By the time the Black Death struck the continent, a gradual shift toward using the vernacular (a country or region's common native language such as English or German) had already begun among scholars and university-trained professionals, including lawyers and physicians. But most historians agree that the use of the vernacular by Europe's educated elite was given an enormous boost by the Great Mortality and the severe depletion in the ranks of those capable of teaching Latin to the rising generation that the pandemic created.

priest. And because priests cannot be found . . . to take on the responsibility for those places and visit the sick and administer the sacraments of the Church to them, . . . we understand that many people are dying without the sacrament of penance [the formal confession of sin, from the Latin word for "repent"]. . . . Therefore, desirous as we must be to provide for the salvation of souls and to call back the wanderers who have strayed from the way, we order and firmly enjoin you, upon your obedience, to make it known speedily and publicly to everybody, but particularly to those who have already fallen sick, that if on the point of death they cannot secure the services of a properly ordained priest, they should make confession of their sins . . . to any lay person, even to a woman, if a man is not available.

CRITICISM OF THE CLERGY

The huge loss of clergymen from the Black Death forced the Catholic leadership to change long-standing church policies regarding the recruitment and ordination of priests. Previously, a man could not be ordained or assume responsibility for a parish church until he reached the age of 25; in the wake of the Great Mortality, Pope Clement VI lowered the age of ordination to just 20 years. Educational requirements for ordination were also relaxed after the Black Death to ensure a larger pool of potential recruits for the priesthood. Since the vast majority of medieval Europeans could not read and depended on their local priest to interpret the Bible for them, this shift in church policy deeply disturbed many Catholics, including the English monk Henry Knighton. For all intents and purposes, grumbled Knighton in his chronicle of the pestilence in Kent, many of the men who "rushed into priestly orders" following the plague were "illiterate, no better than laymen—for even if they could read, they did not understand what they read."

Desperate to fill the thousands of clerical posts left vacant by the plague, church leaders abandoned traditional standards for ordination, recruiting less-experienced and less-educated men to lead congregations than in the past. Many of the novice priests also lacked the high moral standards of their fallen predecessors, according to some critics. In 1350, England's highest-ranking church official, the archbishop of Canterbury, Simon Islap, accused a number of the new ministers—and quite a few of the older, surviving clerics as well—of bringing shame to the church by their "unbridled cupidity" (unrestrained greed). These self-seeking men of the cloth, he complained, were abandoning their assigned congregations to take better-paid positions in the city or as private chaplains to wealthy patrons. In 1351, Pope Clement VI himself blasted the Catholic clergy for straying from the very moral principles they were supposed to be teaching their flocks. "About what can you preach to the people?" he asked. "If on humility, you yourselves are the proudest of the world, arrogant and given to pomp. If on poverty, you are the most grasping and covetous. . . ." Clement's contemporary, the English poet William Langland, agreed with the pope's gloomy assessment of the church's newest recruits. In his famous narrative poem, *Piers Plowman*, he poked bitter fun at greedy and corrupt clergymen who "complained to the bishop/That their parishes were poor since the pestilence year,/Asking license and leave in London to dwell,/To sing there for simony; for silver is sweet. (Simony is the buying or selling of church offices.)

THE GREAT MORTALITY AND RELIGIOUS REFORM

During the decades following the Black Death pandemic, widespread criticism of ill-prepared and corrupt clergymen spurred the growth of several reform movements within the Catholic Church. These included the Fraticelli, a group of

Italian Franciscan monks who viewed poverty as the heart of the Christian life and denounced the church's wealth, and the Lollards, an English sect based on the teachings of Oxford University professor John Wycliffe (also spelled Wyclif), the most influential religious reformer of the Black Death era.

Wycliffe, who was born in Yorkshire, England, about 1320 and died in 1384, lived nearly 200 years before the Protestant Reformation, the great sixteenth-century religious reform movement in western Europe that resulted in the founding of the Protestant churches. Yet Wycliffe's views on church reform had much in common with the ideas of Martin Luther, John Calvin, and other Reformation leaders of the 1500s, prompting some modern scholars to suggest a direct link between the Protestant Reformation and the religious dissent fostered by the Black Death.

Wycliffe not only criticized what he considered as the declining educational and moral standards of the Catholic priesthood in the wake of the Black Death, he also attacked church leadership for increasingly turning to the sale of indulgences (pardons for sinful behavior) and masses for the dead to raise funds during the decades after the Great Mortality. Like Martin Luther and other leaders of the Protestant Reformation, he viewed these practices as fundamentally corrupt and contrary to the teachings of Jesus. Also in common with Luther and later reformers, Wycliffe firmly believed that all Christians should have the opportunity to read the Bible in their own national language, even though Latin had been the official language of the Roman Catholic Church for more than 1,000 years. With the assistance of his followers, the Lollards, Wycliffe produced an English language version of the Holy Scriptures. This infuriated the pope and the rest of the Catholic leadership, who had Wycliffe expelled from his position at Oxford and drove the Lollardy movement underground. Not until 1519, when the German priest Martin Luther penned his famous 95 Theses criticizing church practices and

John Wycliffe (above), the most influential religious figure of the medieval plague era, criticized the Catholic Church for what he viewed as its hypocrisy. Wycliffe was particularly critical of the Church's efforts to raise money through selling masses for the dead and indulgences (pardons for sins) in the aftermath of the Black Death.

teachings, would the religious principles that John Wycliffe had fought for in his plague-ravished homeland finally be resurrected.

THE BLACK DEATH STRIKES THE ART WORLD

The Black Death had as dramatic an impact on the European art world as it did on the European church, carrying away scores of influential artists and highly skilled craftsmen. In some cases, the plague wiped out whole "schools" or guilds of sculptors, painters, and stonemasons, individuals who chose to work together because they favored the same styles or themes. "This not only eliminated some of Europe's greatest masters," wrote Robert Gottfried, "but it made it very difficult to train and develop new talent."

Architecture was especially hard hit by the plague since many of the expert craftsmen needed to create the soaring, lavishly adorned cathedrals that were the centerpiece of medieval architecture perished. Some historians have directly linked the shift in England from the highly ornate Decorated style of church architecture to the plainer Perpendicular style around 1350 to the Black Death.

The loss of large numbers of experienced English and French masons and sculptors during the pandemic made the building of cathedrals in the elaborate decorated style a technical impossibility, these scholars argued, and favored the rise of the more austere perpendicular style of architecture.

MORBID NEW THEMES IN ART

"For the student of the Black Death," wrote historian Joseph Byrne in his book *The Black Death*, "art serves as a window into the past." Although realistic depictions of day-to-day life during the Great Mortality, such as physicians treating patients or mass burials, are rare, dozens of surviving paintings, woodcuts, and sculptures from the Black Death era provide a compelling record of people's psychological responses to the devastating pandemic.

Death was a major theme of medieval art long before the arrival of the Great Mortality. Nonetheless, post-plague European art placed a greater emphasis on death, and particularly its most gruesome and terrifying aspects, than ever before. Grisly depictions of skeletal figures armed with swords and sickles to cut down the living and disemboweled, worm-eaten corpses were common motifs of late fourteenth- and early fifteenth-century art. Perhaps the most popular and famous motif of the era, however, was the Danse Macabre, or Dance of Death.

In the Danse Macabre genre, people representing all occupations and social classes, from kings to servants, nobles to peasants, are "danced away" to their deaths by grinning skeletons or rotting cadavers. The message is clear: Death is the great leveler; it carries off the rich and the poor, the highborn and the humble. Many scholars believe that the Danse Macabre motif first appeared in Germany during or shortly after the Black Death pandemic. By the early fifteenth century, it had spread throughout much of western Europe, including France, where in 1424 the first fresco, or mural, of the Danse Macabre was painted on the wall of the Innocents' cloister in Paris, at that time the site of the city's largest cemetery.

Another famous motif of what author John Kelly calls the "death-obsessed culture of the late Middle Ages," is the transi tomb. For nearly two centuries before the outbreak of the Black Death, prominent Europeans had been commissioning sculptors to create life-size effigies (sculptures) of themselves to adorn their tombs. Yet by the end of the fourteenth century, many of these monuments had taken on a shocking new form. These new transi tombs portrayed the transition or decay of the corpse in hideous detail. For instance, the stone effigy on Cardinal Jean de La Grange's transi tomb in Avignon, France, graphically depicts the decomposing cadaver of the church leader, complete with hollow eye sockets, gaping mouth, and protruding ribs. A grim inscription beneath the sculpture warns visitors: "Let the great and humble, by our example, see to what state they shall be inexorably reduced, whatever their condition, age, or sex. Why then, miserable person, are you puffed up with pride? Dust you are, unto dust you return, rotten corpse, morsel and meal to worms."

THE PLAGUE SAINTS

While the Danse Macabre and transi tomb motifs testify to the profound fear and despair that gripped Europe's plague-ravished population, other favorite artistic themes from the Black Death era testify to the medieval European's intense religious faith. This deep spirituality is particularly evident in the many works of art from the late fourteenth and early fifteenth centuries that portray two Catholic saints who were believed to preserve believers from the plague: St. Sebastian and St. Roch (or Roche).

A high-ranking soldier in the Roman army, St. Sebastian abandoned paganism for Christianity during the late third

century, a period when Christians were being viciously persecuted within the Roman Empire. When the Roman emperor
heard about Sebastian's conversion, he commanded that the
young warrior be tied to a stake and shot with arrows. According to Catholic tradition, Sebastian somehow survived the
torrent of arrows only to be savagely beaten to death by the
emperor's guards.

St. Sebastian's reputation as a protector against pestilence
stems from his miraculous ability to live through a barrage
of arrows. Since biblical days, people had associated arrows
with deadly diseases sent down from heaven to punish sinful
humans. Paintings of St. Sebastian from the Black Death era
typically showed the Christian martyr being pierced by dozens of arrows, many of which have lodged in the same parts of
his body where buboes typically appear on plague victims: the
neck, armpit, and groin areas.

Born into a well-to-do French family around 1300, like
St. Sebastian, St. Roch was a favorite subject of post-plague
religious art. An exceptionally devout young man, Roch was
just 20 years old and on a religious pilgrimage to Rome when
the plague struck Italy. On his way southward through the
Italian Peninsula, Roch stopped in a number of different
communities to minister to the sick. Supposedly, everyone
with whom Roch came into contact made a full recovery from
the deadly disease. After Roch himself contracted the plague,
he withdrew to a remote forest to avoid infecting anyone else.
According to one tradition, a dog kept Roch alive during his
self-imposed exile by bringing him food. On regaining his
health, Roch returned home to France, where he was falsely
accused of being a spy and thrown into prison. When Roch
died in his prison cell five years later, a mysterious letter was
discovered near the corpse. The letter proclaimed that Roch
would intercede with God on behalf of any plague victim who
prayed to him for help. During the decades following the

Black Death, Roch came to be revered throughout Europe as a patron saint of those afflicted by the plague. Medieval paintings typically portray him with a dog by his side and pointing to a large bubo on one of his thighs.

Because arrows were commonly associated with punishments from God, the martyr St. Sebastian was seen as one of the plague saints, a figure Catholics would pray to for help in preventing or curing illness. St. Sebastian miraculously survived a storm of arrows shot by the Roman army as punishment for his Christian beliefs, and was often depicted in paintings wounded by dozens of arrows (above).

THE GREAT MORTALITY AND LITERATURE

The Black Death, most scholars agree, had a significant influence on the literature as well as the art of the late Middle Ages. In his *Canterbury Tales*, Geoffrey Chaucer, the most celebrated writer of the era, emphasized hedonistic (sensual) pleasures and generally sought to amuse and entertain his readers. However, Chaucer, who was probably a child during the Black Death in England, also used the *Canterbury Tales* to criticize what he viewed as the low moral standards of much of the post-plague Catholic clergy, whom he ridiculed as money-grubbers in his famous collection of stories.

After the *Canterbury Tales*, the best-known literary work of the Black Death era was *The Decameron* by Giovanni Boccaccio. Boccaccio, who lost many close friends and family members to the illness, included a detailed and chilling account of the plague in his native Florence in *The Decameron*'s lengthy introduction. The main body of the work, however, consists of a collection of witty and often bawdy tales that 10 young Florentine nobles who have recently fled their plague-ravished hometown for the countryside tell one another to pass the time. Far removed from the somber mood of the book's introduction, the stories' light-hearted tone aptly illustrates the escapist mentality of some of Boccaccio's contemporaries, who sought to drown their anxieties in merrymaking and to live for the moment.

In contrast to Chaucer's and Boccaccio's famous works, much of the literature of the post-plague era was unremittingly melancholy and pessimistic in tone. The prominent French writer Eustace Deschamps (1340?–1404), for instance, once observed gloomily: "Happy is he who has no children, for . . . they give only trouble and anxiety; . . . they are always in danger of falling and hurting themselves; they contract some illness and die. . . . Nothing but cares and sorrows; no happiness compensates us for our anxiety. . . ." A few decades later, an anonymous English poet composed the lugubrious

"Disputation Betwixt the Body and Worms," which features a particularly morbid dialogue between a once beautiful noble-woman and the worms now devouring her rotting corpse:

> The body speaks to the worms:
> *'Worms, worms,' this body said,*
> *'Why do you act thus? What causes you to eat me thus?*
> *By you my flesh is horribly decorated,*
> *Which was once a figure noble and attractive,*
> *Very fragrant and sweet,*
> *Best loved of all creatures*
> *Called lady and sovereign, I assure you'. . .*
>
>
> Worms speak to the body:
> *'Nay, nay! We will not yet depart from you*
> *Not while one of your bones hangs with another,*
> *'Til we have scoured and polished them*
> *And made everything between them as clean as we can.*
> *For our labor we ask to extract nothing,*
> *Not riches of gold or silver, nor any other reward*
> *But only for we worms to feed on you.'*

The moral of this gruesome tale, the poem's author declared, was unmistakable: "When you least expect it, death comes to conquer you." Therefore, the poet admonishes his readers, "It is good to think on death." Clearly, his was a message that the death-obsessed culture of late medieval Europe had already taken to heart.

The End of the Black Death

By 1352, the Black Death had faded away from most of Europe except for northwestern Russia. The plague was not yet finished with the continent, however. Over the course of the next three-and-a-half centuries, periodic outbreaks of bubonic plague would continue to vex the people of Europe.

THE DISAPPEARANCE OF PLAGUE FROM EUROPE

From the late 1300s through the early 1600s, the plague visited Europe repeatedly but never with the ferocity of the mid-fourteenth-century pandemic. Although France continued to suffer occasional plague outbreaks until the 1720s, in 1665 and 1666 the disease made its final big strike in Europe when the Great Plague of London claimed an estimated 70,000 lives. Some historians believe that the Great Fire of London of September 1666, which consumed more than 13,000 houses and other buildings, put an abrupt end to the epidemic by incinerating much of the city's plague-bearing rodent and flea populations.

Following an outbreak in the Mediterranean port city of Marseille, France, in 1722, the plague effectively withdrew from Europe. Scientists and historians have suggested a number of different theories to explain this turn of events. Some researchers have stressed the replacement of the oriental rat flea's favorite host, the black rat (*Rattus rattus*), throughout much of Europe by the larger brown rat (*Rattus norvegicus*), which the plague-bearing fleas normally shun. Others have suggested that the microorganism behind the plague, *Y. pestis*, gradually evolved into a less lethal form during the centuries following the Black Death. Recently, however, many scholars, including historian William H. McNeill, have concluded that changes in human behavior were probably the key factor in the disappearance of the plague from Europe.

In his book *Plagues and Peoples*, McNeill argues that important changes in how Europeans coexisted with plague-carrying rats and fleas were central to the disease's departure from the continent. By the late 1600s, solid brick and stone dwellings were replacing traditional wood or wattle and daub (twig and mud) homes in many parts of Europe. At the same time, less flammable slate or tile roofs were being substituted for thatch ones. These changes, McNeill writes, "tended to increase the distance between rodent and human occupants of the dwelling, making it more difficult for a flea to transfer from a dying rat to a susceptible human. Thatch roofs, in particular, offered ready refuge for rats; and it was easy for a flea to fall from such a roof onto someone beneath. When thatch roofs were replaced by tiles, . . . opportunities for this kind of transfer of infection drastically diminished."

In addition to changes in housing materials and construction, better public sanitation such as sewers and garbage control probably contributed to the plague's disappearance from the continent by decreasing local rodent populations, many scholars believe. Improved personal hygiene among all groups of Europeans during the seventeenth and eighteenth centuries may also have helped seal the plague's fate on the continent by keeping disease-carrying fleas away from the human population.

THE PLAGUE STRIKES
EAST ASIA AND CALIFORNIA

After withdrawing from the European continent during the early eighteenth century, the plague largely faded from the world scene until the late nineteenth century, when it struck the impoverished Asian countries of China and India with a vengeance during what is generally known as the Third Plague Pandemic. (The First Pandemic was the Plague of Justinian that hit the Mediterranean region during the sixth century; the Second Pandemic was the Black Death.) The Third Pandemic finally petered out during the 1940s, but not before

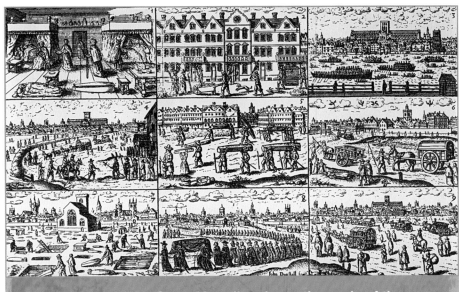

This depiction of the Great Mortality shows the scale of the plague, and how it affected individuals, neighborhoods, and entire cities. As people fell victim to illness, mass graves were dug and entire populations attempted to flee infected cities, spreading the plague even further into Europe.

claiming millions of lives and making appearances in seaports all over the globe.

Soon after the turn of the twentieth century, the Third Pandemic briefly visited the United States, striking the bustling port city of San Francisco. The illness almost certainly arrived in the Bay area on a Chinese ship, which turned out to be harboring two plague-stricken stowaways along with numerous *Y. pestis*–infected rats and fleas, no doubt. Between 1900 and 1904, 121 cases of plague were confirmed in San Francisco; 113 of the victims, most of whom were residents of the rat-infested Chinatown district, died.

On April 18, 1906, almost exactly two years after the last case of bubonic plague had been reported in San Francisco, a massive earthquake devastated the city, leaving hundreds of thousands homeless. The rat and flea population exploded, and plague once again flared up in the city, infecting a total of 160 residents and killing 77. The death toll would surely have been higher if not for an ambitious sanitation campaign launched by city officials in 1908. More than a million rats were trapped and slaughtered during the campaign, and by the end of the year, the plague had departed San Francisco for good. The last sizable plague outbreak to ever hit the United States also occurred in California, when at least 30 people, most of them Mexican migrant workers, died of pneumonic plague in Los Angeles in late 1924 and early 1925.

THE PLAGUE SINCE THE DEVELOPMENT OF ANTIBIOTICS

During the 1940s, the development of antibiotic drugs capable of destroying *Y. pestis* and other disease-causing bacteria revolutionized the medical world and made plague a highly treatable illness for the first time ever. Since the development of potent antibiotic drugs such as streptomycin and tetracycline, the vast majority of plague deaths have been linked to delays in diagnosis and treatment of the disease. Before the advent of antibiotics, bubonic plague victims had a mortality rate of between 50 and 60 percent; after the drugs were introduced, the mortality rate plummeted to approximately 5 percent. In the rarer and more lethal pneumonic form of plague, patients who receive the appropriate antibiotics within 24 hours of infection have a mortality rate of just 15–20 percent, compared to a 95–100 percent mortality rate before the development of the drugs.

Today, the *Y. pestis* bacillus still exists in the environment in many parts of the world. Plague reservoirs—areas where the plague bacterium occurs naturally within the animal population, have been identified in Asia, Africa, and the Americas. Scientists now know that more than 200 species of animals can serve as plague carriers, including squirrels, chipmunks, prairie dogs, deer mice, and rabbits, in addition to rats. Although the oriental rat flea, *X. cheopis*, is still the chief transmitter of the plague to humans, so far 30 different flea species have been identified as potential plague vectors.

Since the 1960s, an average of about 1,500 plague cases per year have been reported worldwide. The illness is most common in the developing nations of Asia and Africa, where antibiotic drugs are often hard to obtain, and sanitation conditions are typically substandard. In the United States, only about 10 to 15 plague cases are reported each year, the vast majority of them in rural areas of the West.

THE MOST FEARED DISEASE IN HUMAN HISTORY?

Due in large measure to the widely studied and extraordinarily lethal Black Death pandemic of the mid-1300s, the plague may be the most famous—and feared—disease in human history. Even today, more than six-and-a-half centuries after the Black Death, the specter of a major plague outbreak still haunts the world.

Since the late twentieth century, and especially since the attack on the World Trade Center in New York City on

September 11, 2001, many public health experts have voiced concern regarding the use of plague as an agent of bioterrorism or biowarfare. Since it is the only plague strain that can be readily passed from person to person, the most likely scenario would involve pneumonic plague bacteria, converted into aerosol form and sprayed over heavily populated areas. In response to the possibility of such an attack, local and national health officials in the United States maintain large supplies of *Y. pestis*–killing antibiotics, supplies that can be rushed to any part of the country in a matter of hours. Given the ready availability of potent antibiotic drugs, there is no reason to believe that the human race will ever again have to endure a bubonic or pneumonic plague catastrophe on the scope of the Black Death. Nonetheless, the recent discovery of an antibiotic-resistant strain of *Y. pestis* on the African island of Madagascar has brought a new sense of urgency to research aimed at preventing and controlling the disease that brought so much suffering to the medieval world.

Chronology

c. 541	Plague of Justinian, probably bubonic plague, strikes throughout the Mediterranean region.
1315	Great Famine begins in northern Europe and British Isles.
c. 1320s–1330s	Black Death begins in central Asia and starts spreading outward.
1337	Hundred Years' War between England and France starts.
1346	Crimean port of Kaffa is besieged by Mongols, who reportedly use plague-infested corpses as weapons.
1347	Black Death arrives in Sicily from the Crimea aboard Italian merchant ships.
1348	Black Death spreads into Italy first, then sweeps through much of western and central Europe, including England; flagellant movement begins; Jews are persecuted.
1349	Black Death arrives in Scotland and Scandinavia; Pope Clement VI publicly condemns flagellants; British government issues Ordinance of Laborers.
1350	Black Death reaches eastern Europe and Greenland.
1351	British government institutes Statute of Laborers.

1352	Black Death arrives in Moscow, Russia, but has largely faded throughout most of the rest of Europe.
1353	Giovanni Boccaccio finishes writing *The Decameron*.
1358	French peasant uprising, the Jacquerie.
1381	Peasants' Revolt in England.
1665–1666	Great Plague of London kills an estimated 70,000.
1894	Alexandre Yersin identifies the bacterium that causes bubonic plague dur-

Timeline

c. 1320s-1330s
Black Death begins in central Asia and starts spreading outward.

1348
Black Death spreads into Italy first, then sweeps through much of western and central Europe, including England; flagellant movement begins; Jews are persecuted.

1320

1348

1346
Crimean port of Kaffa is besieged by Mongols, who reportedly use plague-infested corpses as weapons.

1347
Black Death arrives in Sicily from the Crimea aboard Italian merchant ships.

ing a plague pandemic in East Asia; bubonic plague begins to be linked to the Black Death.

1990   Reappearance of plague in humans on the African island of Madagascar.

1995   First multidrug-resistant strain of *Y. pestis* isolated in 1995.

1349
Black Death arrives in Scotland and Scandinavia.

1351–1352
Black Death arrives in Moscow but has largely faded throughout most of the rest of Europe.

1995
First multidrug-resistant strain of *Y. pestis* isolated in 1995.

1350

1995

1350
Black Death reaches eastern Europe and Greenland.

1894
Alexandre Yersin identifies the bacterium that causes bubonic plague during a plague pandemic in Asia; bubonic plague begins to be linked to the Black Death.

Glossary

astrology   Considered a branch of science during the Middle Ages, astrology studies the supposed effect of the heavenly bodies—particularly the planets, Moon, and stars—on the Earth and on human affairs.

bacillus   A rod-shaped bacterium (the singular form of the word *bacteria*). The bacillus *Yersinia pestis (Y. pestis)* causes bubonic, septicemic, and pneumonic plague.

buboes   The black bulges that develop in or near the groin, neck, and armpits of bubonic plague victims. Buboes result from the accumulation of bacteria and dead cells in the lymph nodes, which are reservoirs in the body where such impurities collect.

bubonic plague   A frequently deadly disease caused by the bacillus *Y. pestis*. Transmitted by the bite of fleas from an infected rodent, usually a rat, bubonic plague is characterized by weakness; high fever; rapid pulse rate; and painful, swollen lymph nodes (buboes).

Danse Macabre   A popular artistic motif of the Black Death era that portrayed death as a skeleton or rotting corpse dancing away plague victims from all social classes and occupations to their deaths.

epidemic   A disease that spreads rapidly and widely.

feudalism   In many parts of medieval Europe, feudalism was the hierarchy of power by which every level of society had certain obligations to the level above it.

flagellants   Catholic Christians who whipped themselves and each other in public in an effort to appease God's anger with humankind's sinfulness.

Golden Horde   A branch of the Mongols, a central Asian people who carved out a huge empire during the Middle Ages stretching from China to Hungary; the Golden Horde ruled Russia on the eve of the Black Death.

guild   An association of skilled craftsmen, artists, or merchants organized to uphold standards and to safeguard the interests of its membership.

hemorrhaging   A common symptom of the relatively rare but highly deadly septicemic plague; hemorrhaging is profuse bleeding resulting from ruptured blood vessels.

humors   According to the second-century Greco-Roman physician Galen, the four substances that flowed through the human body: phlegm, blood, yellow bile, and black bile. Medieval physicians believed that when the four humors became unbalanced, illness resulted.

Lollards   Members of a sect of Catholic religious reformers in post–Black Death England who followed the teachings of the Oxford professor and biblical scholar John Wycliffe.

lymph nodes   Part of the lymphatic system, lymph nodes are small masses of tissue that help to filter out impurities from the tissues.

lymphatic system   The network of vessels and nodes that circulate lymph throughout the body. Lymph is a watery fluid that rids tissues of bacteria, dead cells, and other impurities. The lymphatic system helps the body defend itself against disease and maintains bodily fluids in balance.

monoculture   The growing of just one crop.

miasma   Poisonous vapors that supposedly seeped out of rotting corpses and swamps, among other sources.

Miasma was considered as a chief cause of disease by medieval physicians.

microorganisms   Living creatures too tiny to be seen with the naked eye.

Middle Ages   The era in European history that is commonly dated from the fall of the Roman Empire in about 400 to the dawn of the great cultural revival known as the Renaissance in approximately 1400.

pandemic   An outbreak of disease over a large geographical area and affecting a high percentage of the population.

pestilence   A deadly epidemic disease.

plague reservoir   A geographical area where *Y. pestis*, the bacillus that causes bubonic, pneumonic, and septicemic plague, occurs naturally within the wild rodent population.

pneumonic plague   A highly lethal form of plague in which the bacillus *Y. pestis* invades the lungs. Unlike bubonic plague, it can be spread from person to person through the air.

pogroms   Organized, large-scale attacks on Jews.

***Rattus rattus* (*R. rattus*)**   Also known as the black or house rat, a principal vector or transmitter for the bubonic plague along with *X. cheopis*, the oriental rat flea.

septicemic plague   A highly fatal form of plague in which the bacillus *Y. pestis* enters the bloodstream, causing blood vessels to hemorrhage and severely damaging vital organs.

serfs   During the Middle Ages, peasants who were tied to their lord's estates or manors and owed him certain labor obligations and other dues in exchange for protection and the use of some of his land for themselves.

steppes   The vast, dry grasslands of central Asia where the Black Death pandemic is widely thought to have originated.

sumptuary laws Aimed at reinforcing traditional divisions between medieval Europe's social classes, sumptuary laws specified what styles of clothes could be worn by non-nobles in an effort to prevent newly wealthy commoners from trying to imitate their social "betters" following the Black Death.

theriac Supposed antidotes for the plague "poison" made of mashed or finely chopped snake meat along with such other exotic ingredients as powdered gold, seed pearls, and coral.

transi tomb Tombs decorated with effigies or sculptures that portray the transition or decay of the deceased's body in graphic detail.

vector An organism that serves as a carrier for a disease-producing microorganism.

vernacular A country or region's common native language.

Xenopsylla cheopis (*X. cheopis*) Also known as the oriental rat flea, a principal vector for bubonic plague along with its favorite rat host, the black or house rat, *R. rattus*.

Yersinia pestis (*Y. pestis*) Named for Alexandre Yersin, the Swiss-born biologist who isolated and identified it, *Y. pestis* is the bacillus that causes bubonic, septicemic, and pneumonic plague.

Bibliography

Aberth, John. *From the Brink of the Apocalypse: Confronting Famine, War, Plague, and Death in the Later Middle Ages*. New York: Routledge, 2001.

Benedictow, Ole J. "The Black Death." *History Today* March 2005.

Boccaccio, Giovanni. *The Decameron*. Trans. G.H. McWilliam. Harmondsworth, U.K.: Penguin, 1972.

Byrne, Joseph P. *The Black Death*. Westport, Conn.: Greenwood Press, 2004.

Cantor, Norman F. *In the Wake of the Plague: The Black Death and the World It Made*. New York: HarperCollins, 2002.

———."Europe: 1348: Plague and Economics." *The Economist* December 31, 1999, p. 33, 36.

Gottfried, Robert S. *The Black Death: Natural and Human Disaster in Medieval Europe*. New York: The Free Press, 1983.

Herlihy, David. *The Black Death and the Transformation of the West*. Cambridge, Mass.: Harvard University Press, 1997.

Kelly, John. *The Great Mortality: An Intimate History of the Black Death, the Most Devastating Plague of All Time*. New York: HarperCollins, 2005.

Marriott, Edward. *Plague: A Story of Science, Rivalry, and the Scourge That Won't Go Away*. New York: Henry Holt, 2002.

McKitterick, Rosamond. *Atlas of the Medieval World*. New York: Oxford University Press, 2004.

McNeill, William H. *Plagues and Peoples*. New York: Doubleday, 1977.

Nardo, Don, ed. *The Black Death*. San Diego: Greenhaven, 1999.

Scott, Susan, and Christopher Duncan. *The Return of the Black Death: The World's Greatest Serial Killer*. Hoboken, N.J.: Chichester, 2004.

Tuchman, Barbara W. *A Distant Mirror: The Calamitous Fourteenth Century*. New York: Alfred A. Knopf, 1978.

Wheelis, Mark. "Biological Warfare at the 1346 Siege of Caffa." *Emerging Infectious Diseases* September 2002, pp. 971–975.

Ziegler, Philip. *The Black Death*. London: Collins, 1969.

WEB SITES

Decameron Web: The Plague
http://www.brown.edu/Departments/Italian_Studies/dweb/
plague/index.shtml

The Great Mortality
http://historymedren.about.com/od/theblackdeath/a/great
mortality.htm

The Middle Ages
http://www.themiddleages.net/

The Middle Ages: The Black Death
http://history.boisestate.edu/westciv/plague/

Further Reading

DeHahn, Tracee. *The Black Death*. Philadelphia: Chelsea House, 2002.

Dunn, John M. *Life During the Black Death*. San Diego: Lucent, 2000.

Giblin, James Cross. *When Plague Strikes: The Black Death, Small-pox, AIDS*. New York: HarperCollins, 1995.

Konstam, Angus. *Atlas of Medieval Europe*. New York: Checkmark, 2000.

McCabe, Suzanne. "Dark Death." *Junior Scholastic* February 11, 2002, pp. 18–20.

McMullin, Jordan, ed. *The Black Death*. San Diego: Greenhaven, 2003.

Picture Credits

Page:

8: © Infobase Publishing

13: © HIP/Art Resource, NY

21: © Erich Lessing/Art Resource, NY

24: © Camerphoto Arte, Venice/ Art Resource, NY

26: © Hulton Archive/Getty Images

34: © SMC Images/Getty Images

39: © Time & Life Pictures/ Getty Images

42: © Time & Life Pictures/ Getty Images

54: © Erich Lessing/Art Resource, NY

61: © Image Select/Art Resource, NY

67: © HIP/ Art Resource, NY

70: © Hulton Archive/Getty Images

74: © Giraudon/Art Resource, NY

80: © Snark/Art Resource, NY

89: © HIP/Art Resource, NY

93: © DeA Picture Library/ Art Resource, NY

98: © HIP/ Art Resource, NY

102: © François Guenet/Art Resource, NY

107: © HIP/Art Resource, NY

Index

About the Author

LOUISE CHIPLEY SLAVICEK received her master's degree in history from the University of Connecticut. She is the author of numerous periodical articles and 20 books for young adults, including *Women of the American Revolution*, *Israel*, and *The Great Wall of China*. She lives in Ohio with her husband, James, a research biologist, and their two children, Krista and Nathan.